Contents

Introduction

It had been one of those days. My middle-school students had to be dragged kicking and screaming through the writing we were doing. When I got home, I sank into my comfy chair and thumbed through the pieces they had turned in—dismal. What was I missing? Why couldn't these fascinating, energetic, and talkative young students bring their interests and passion for life to their writing?

Next to my chair were a couple of shelves of books my son, Sam, and I had read and loved when he was little, including *Green Eggs and Ham* by Dr. Seuss, *The Little Engine That Could* by Watty Piper, and *The Little House* by Virginia Lee Burton. I picked one up and started to read. Then another and another, until it hit me. These books, these wonderful picture books, had that very energy that was missing in my students' work. They were short, carefully crafted, and perfect examples of what good writing looks like. I gathered my favorites together and took them to school the next day.

When I passed the picture books out, the students were shocked. "These are baby books!" they cried. After a few minutes, though, they began to read. Amidst comments such as, "Oh, I remember this one—I loved it when I was little" and "You have to read this. It's the best ever," we began to notice the details of the craft that made each book so memorable. A great lead, delicious words, logical organization, powerful voice, fluid sentences, and fully developed ideas—all were within the short span of a picture book. Their conventions were virtually flawless, and their presentations—though widely varied from one text to the next—were inviting, pleasing, and sometimes flat-out awesome. Not coincidentally, the qualities we noticed matched right up with the traits of writing we'd been using to frame our discussions of writing. A revelation! Discovering the traits in picture books breathed new life into our writing endeavors.

From that day on we were hooked. When I overheard one of my students say, "I wish I could write like this," I knew we were onto something great. The students and I began to collect picture books that we thought were well-written and inspirational. We cleared our classroom library's shelves and started categorizing the books by their strongest writing trait: ideas, organization, voice, word choice, sentence fluency, conventions, or presentation.

Picture books became one of my most important teaching tools. When they were stuck, students voluntarily went to them for ideas and examples of what to do with their writing. Over time, I started seeing the influence of these texts in their writing. I often overheard comments and bits of advice from one student to another about how these books could help improve their pieces.

- "Read *Bat Loves the Night*. That's how you want your sentences to sound."
- "Get creative with an old idea like David Wisniewski does in *The Secret Knowledge of Grown-Ups*."
- "If you want readers to like your piece, it's got to have voice like Elizabeth Winthrop's *Dumpy La Rue*."
- "Have some fun with the words like in *The Web Files*."
- "Bring your sports stories to life like Robert Burleigh does in *Goal*."

After adding picture books to my toolbox, my students' writing improved. Their work got better all the way around—and they had a lot more fun creating it. Finding that picture books could be used to teach writing to students of any age was one of my greatest, most delightful discoveries.

Picture books provide a highly visual way to engage students in reading and writing. They deal with almost any topic imaginable, so you are bound to find picture books that will appeal to all your students. Who can resist the beautiful prose in *A Day's Work* where the grandfather teaches his grandson, Francisco, an important lesson in integrity? Or how can you put down *Bullfrog Pops!*, a delightful romp that invites the reader to predict what happens, and never fails to surprise? Young readers can appreciate books like these at a literal level. Older readers who understand a subtle bit of humor or a powerful subtext can appreciate these books at a deeper level. These works serve as marvelous models for our student writers—no matter what their age is.

In addition to traditional picture books, there are "micro texts," which have more text on each page, more sophisticated story lines, and riskier presentations. Micro texts are a far cry from the early picture books I first used with my middle-school students. These books are being written with older audiences in mind and are much loved and appreciated.

- Micro texts can be used as examples to spark the imagination. Use *The Secret Knowledge of Grown-Ups,* for example, to create student texts that have original and clever ideas such as those found in David Wisniewski's book.

- Micro texts can be used to inspire new forms and formats for writing. *The Spider and the Fly* by Tony DiTerlizzi and *The Magic Fan* by Keith Baker are not only beautifully written, but a pleasure to look at as well. Collect visually appealing books for students to study and admire as they plan how to organize and present their own final, finished copy.

- Micro texts can be used as examples of outstanding nonfiction writing right along with their fiction counterparts. From the biography of Babe Ruth, *The Babe & I* by David Adler, to understanding how a cell forms in *Blood & Gore* by Vicki Cobb, students will learn how to present factual information with lively, engaging voice by referring to models as they write.

Once you begin to collect picture books, you may find it addictive. You might begin with a favorite title that goes with a unit or particular lesson from your curriculum. Then you find another. A student brings in another. A colleague suggests another that fits exactly what you are studying—and you are on your way. You will find these books serve as teaching tools for each trait, and you'll want more to serve as models to inspire your student writers.

About This Book

This book contains more than 200 annotations of high-quality picture books and suggests ways to use those books to spark lessons to help students develop skills in each of the seven writing traits. In every high-quality picture book, you'll find these traits working in harmony, but often, individual traits just seem to jump out. For example, *The Hickory Chair* by Lisa Rowe Fraustino is perfect for teaching students how to use a specific detail to develop a bigger theme. Rowe Fraustino uses the notes the grandmother leaves behind upon her death as a way to explore the timelessness of family love and that very special grandparent and grandchild relationship.

The books in this bibliography were discovered through recommendations from teachers and students, by checking award lists, from endless hours of bookstore haunting, and sometimes by sheer good luck. Most of these titles were published in the past five years, but some are classics that just had to be included to round out the list. To make the list, the book had to have the makings of a text that students could use to learn something about one or more of the traits.

The book is organized by trait. Each chapter contains a list of annotated picture books that exemplify use of the trait and focus lessons that show how to use some of those books to inspire use of the trait. These focus lessons come from talented elementary, middle-school, and even high-school teachers all over the country. No matter what grade you teach, you are bound to find some interesting books to add to your collection—and new ideas for using those books to inspire young writers.

In assembling this collection, the picture books themselves told me which trait they go with, but as you read them yourself, and share them with your students, you may find other traits to use a particular title for as well. Go for it! The suggestions in this book are just that—suggestions. A place to get started. Traits in picture books are easy to spot, and easy to teach.

Some Background on the Traits

In case you are unfamiliar with the traits of writing, here is a quick review of them:

Ideas: the meaning and development of the message

Organization: the internal structure of the piece

Voice: the way the writer brings the topic to life

Word Choice: the specific vocabulary the writer uses to convey meaning

Sentence Fluency: the way the words and phrases flow throughout the text

Conventions: the mechanical correctness of the piece

Presentation: the overall appearance of the work

A detailed description of each trait, guidelines for assessing student writing according to the traits, and ideas for teaching writing according to the traits can be found in *The 6+1 Traits of Writing: The Complete Guide* by Ruth Culham (Scholastic, 2003). You'll also find a history of the traits, their development over the years at Northwest Regional Educational Laboratory in Portland, Oregon, and research showing the effectiveness of the traits as a writing assessment and instruction tool.

The traits provide the common vocabulary that writers use as they work to create interesting and informative texts. They guide revision and editing. Think of it—what better way to teach how to write an effective introduction (which is part of the organization trait) than to lay out a sampling of picture books and study their introductions? Students can make a list of the different ways these books begin, and then pick a model that they think works well and try it in their own writing. Or perhaps you have noticed that students are having a hard time with sentence fluency. Their writing is choppy or awkward. Or it is just the opposite; it contains endless run-on sentences. A handful of picture books, read aloud to emphasize their exquisitely crafted phrasing, might be just what students need as a model for their own work. Tired of hearing, "I don't know what to write about?" Show students picture books that illustrate how ideas can come from everyday events, and how authors get inside those events to present their unique perspective.

And voice. What a glorious way to teach voice. Good picture books are loaded with voice, from ones that make us cry (Thank you, Patricia Polacco), to ones that make us laugh (Thank you, Doreen Cronin), to the ones that that inspire us so greatly that we feel the hairs on the back of our necks stand on end (Thank you, Jon Muth).

Using picture books to help students of all ages become better writers is an effective strategy. Whether this idea is new to you or you've already embraced it, I hope this resource will help to make your writing trait classroom more effective.

Picture Books for All Ages

> "The picture book is a peculiar art form that thrives on genius, intuition, daring, and a meticulous attention to its history and its various, complex components. The picture book is a picture puzzle, badly misunderstood by critics and condescended to by far too many as merely a trifle for 'the kiddies.'"
>
> –Maurice Sendak
> from the foreword to *George and Martha: The Complete Stories of Two Best Friends*

Picture books can inspire deep thinking and meaningful writing for readers of all ages. Although *Through the Cracks* by Carolyn Sollman, Barbara Emmons, and Judith Paolini is written for children, I have found that educators—teachers, administrators, and staff developers—embrace its ideas and are inspired by its timely message. This is a book you will want to share with your colleagues right along with your students.

Through the Cracks is a cleverly illustrated story about how dismal a school can be when it doesn't work. Told through the eyes of one student—literally shrunk to the size where she can fall "through the cracks" of the school floor—it reminds us all that schools should be places where the needs of students come first, where activities are stimulating, where learning is celebrated. If you have colleagues who doubt the power of using picture books with older students, this book may turn them around. It's that powerful. I'm convinced that adding it to every professional library will promote passionate discussions about where we fail students and how we have to do better. I invite every teacher and administrator to read this book and talk about its message. I encourage teachers to share it with students and ask them if they have ever felt like the youngsters in this story. Then, listen and take note. I use the following lesson with teacher educators; it can be easily adapted for students.

Focus Lesson Based On . . .

Through the Cracks

Carolyn Sollman, Barbara Emmons, and Judith Paolini, Authors

Sterling Publishing, 1994

(See description on page 25.)

Target Trait: Ideas
Secondary Trait: Voice

Materials:

- A copy of *Through the Cracks* for each participant
- Blank overhead transparencies and wipe-off pens
- Large butcher paper or chart paper
- Markers

What to Do:

1. Before reading the book, ask participants to talk about times in their lives when they felt they fell "through the cracks." Perhaps it was an experience involving big government bureaucracy or an incident at school.

2. On an overhead transparency, record their experiences and how they made them feel.

Example:

A time I felt like I had fallen "through the cracks":	**How it made me feel:**
1. When I was a student in high school classes with forty other classmates.	**1.** I felt like it didn't matter if I was there or not.
2. When the army "lost" my discharge orders.	**2.** I was frustrated and I felt powerless. I was supposed to be going home, but I was stuck on base for another six weeks.
3. When the airlines lost my luggage.	**3.** I felt angry. My vacation was not off to a good start.
4.	**4.**
5.	**5.**

3. Discuss these observations with the group.
4. Give each person a copy of *Through the Cracks*.
5. Divide the whole group into smaller groups of no more than five.
6. Ask members from each group to take turns reading the book aloud and stopping to observe the illustrations.
7. Be sure groups spend time on the second page (the picture of the neighborhood) and look for all the things that are going wrong.
8. Then, at the end of the reading, have them pause to notice the picture of the neighborhood at the text's conclusion and think about and discuss how it's different from the picture at the beginning.
9. Bring the group back together and discuss reactions to the book—positive and negative.
10. On the butcher paper or chart paper, ask participants to record where in their schools students might feel like they fall "through the cracks." Ask them to brainstorm solutions to each scenario.

Example:

Where students fall "through the cracks" at our school:

1. Students have six different teachers every day.
2. We don't have as many elective/activity classes as we used to after the budget cuts.
3. Students are reading because they have to, not because they want to. They just don't seem to enjoy it.
4. Students don't write as well as we think they could. They don't seem to care about their writing.

What we can do about it:

1. Make sure that all teachers talk to students in the hallways as well as their classroom, using their names.
2. Parents and other community members can come and offer music, P.E., and drama activities to students before school, at lunch, and after school.
3. Try adding picture books as a motivator to read up to more challenging works about the same ideas.
4. Try adding picture books as a way to show students the craft of writing interesting pieces that show strengths in all the traits.

11. Once all the ideas are recorded, ask the group to predict how they think students would react to this same exercise.

12. Discuss how to use this book with students and plan a lesson that will encourage students to share ideas on making learning more interesting at school.

Follow Up:

- Carry out the lesson in your classroom.
- Create an action plan that students can work on with staff to make learning more interesting and dynamic at their school.
- Read Sharon Creech's *A Fine, Fine School* (HarperCollins, 2001), another book on the same topic, for additional food for thought and discussion.

CHAPTER ONE

Inspiring Ideas

"We need to consider picture books as literature—not children's literature—but as *literature*."

—Thomas Newkirk
Beyond Words: Picture Books for Older Readers and Writers

One of the hardest things about writing is figuring out what you want to say. Oh sure, there are many professional resources out there that offer suggestions for teaching students how to find topics, narrow them, and add details. Lots of those resources are helpful. A good teacher considers all tools that serve to improve her practice. Now add this one: picture books. No matter how old the writer, no matter how stuck the student may be to find a good topic, extraordinary picture books provide inspiration. From playing baseball to watching whales, from visiting Grandma to visiting the Grand Canyon, from being lost to being found, these books serve as wonderful models of how to work with an idea and make it real to the reader.

Ideas: A Definition

In the simplest of terms, ideas make up the content of the piece. When the ideas are strong, the overall message is clear, not garbled. For students to arrive at good content, we must help them:

- Select an idea (the topic—sometimes assigned, sometimes not)
- Narrow the idea (focus)
- Elaborate on the idea (development)
- Discover the best information to convey the main idea (details)

In the process, students internalize the skills of good writers. They begin to move from general to specific. They notice what others overlook. They describe the bits and pieces of life, the ordinary, in extraordinary ways. Once this happens, they are on their way. They have something important to say in their writing that no one else does. Their ideas come alive. Imagine!

Feature Focus Lesson Based On . . .

Nothing Ever Happens on 90th Street
Roni Schotter, Author
Krysten Brooker, Illustrator
Orchard Books, 1997
(See description on page 24.)

Target Trait: Ideas
Secondary Traits: Organization, Voice

In this marvelously energetic tale, the author addresses the age-old complaint: "I have nothing to write about." Young Eva wanders through her neighborhood looking for things to write about for a class assignment and, as she goes, everyone from the fish salesman to the limousine driver offers delightful words of wisdom. The result is a picture book that could be the focus of an entire course on writing.

MATERIALS:

- A copy of *Nothing Ever Happens on 90th Street*
- A checklist of stations that students will visit
- Bookbinding supplies: large white paper, magazines to cut up, markers, pens, pencils, glue, tape, scissors

WHAT TO DO:

1. Read aloud and discuss *Nothing Ever Happens on 90th Street.*

2. Give students a checklist of at least twelve stations around the school and tell them to check off each one as they visit it for no more than two minutes. Here is what your checklist might look like:

    - *Take a seat inside the media center.*
    - *Hang out in the music room.*
    - *Sit at a table in the cafeteria.*
    - *Check out the action in the back foyer.*
    - *Watch a class in the gym.*
    - *See what is happening in the art room.*
    - *Relax on a bench outside the office.*
    - *Observe a first- or second-grade classroom.*
    - *Visit a classroom you've never been to before.*
    - *Follow the secretary or the custodian for two minutes.*
    - *Observe a class at recess.*
    - *Count the number of cars that pull in and out of the parking lot every two minutes.*

3. Stagger where students start and request that they follow the sequence of stations on their checklist to avoid overcrowding at individual stations. Encourage them to work on their own while they record information about each place—the sights, the sounds, the feel, and the people.

4. Encourage students to gather two or three interesting details about their observations at each station and record them on their checklist. Tell them they can illustrate their

details, just like Eva did in the story. Remind them to be "invisible" and courteous during their visits and to follow the advice of Eva's 90th Street neighbors who suggested:

- Write about what you know.
- Observe carefully and don't neglect the details.
- Find the poetry: a new way with old words.
- Use your imagination.
- Ask, "What if?"
- Add a little action.

5. Have students share their details when they return to the classroom.

6. Have students write "Nothing Ever Happens at (the name of your school) . . ." stories of their own. From there, ask them to illustrate and create bound books to display in the media center for schoolmates to enjoy. Be sure to put a copy of Schotter's book next to the student-written books so readers will see how picture books inspire good writing.

FOLLOW UP:

- Ask students to repeat this exercise at home, noting all the little things that they notice about everyday life on their street.

Picture Books for Inspiring Ideas

Mama Played Baseball

David A. Adler, Author

Chris O'Leary, Illustrator

Harcourt, 2003

Point of view is a tricky concept to teach. Establishing and refining a character's point of view in a story can be challenging to young writers. This is the true story of a player in the first professional women's baseball league, told by her greatest fan, her daughter. As the reader hears about the challenges and hurdles in this woman's life, her daughter's point of view is revealed through her pride in both her parents' accomplishments: one in the military, and the other a mother and pro baseball player during World War II.

The Polar Express

Chris Van Allsburg, Author and Illustrator

Houghton Mifflin, 1985

This marvelous tale of magic and imagination is bound to put a twinkle in even the most cynical eye. As the reader moves through the tale of a boy's trip to the North Pole on Christmas Eve, the words and imagery create a sense of wonder. The idea behind this book is simple . . . yet never fails to inspire multilayered discussion and writing. See if your students can sum up the theme in just one sentence! Then let them explain.

Anno's Mysterious Multiplying Jar

Masaichiro and Mitsumasa Anno, Authors

Mitsumasa Anno, Illustrator

Philomel Books, 1983

This fascinating book is a math teacher's dream. Moving from the concrete to the abstract, it dives into the concept of factoring. A related chapter book entitled *The Number Devil* by Hans Enzensberger is also worth checking out. Both books capture the reader's imagination by exploring concepts one at a time through words and pictures. Math was never so intriguing!

A. Lincoln and Me

Louise Borden, Author

Ted Lewin, Illustrator

Scholastic, 1999

I'm always on the hunt for well-written and interesting nonfiction. Although this is a story, it is based on facts and is an excellent example of how to organize facts and present them in a form that makes them engaging to read. The use of parallel information is another noteworthy feature: for example, the narrator, a young boy, talks about all the things he and Abraham Lincoln share, including a birthday. Students will learn about Lincoln while relating to information about the narrator. Use this book as a model for students to write their own nonfiction pieces about other noteworthy historical figures.

Fireflies!

Julie Brinckloe, Author and Illustrator

Aladdin Paperbacks, 1985

This magical little piece is sure to delight. Sometimes the smallest moments in a story are what make it special. This book celebrates one of those moments, focusing the reader on the significance of an important life lesson—that sometimes in order to keep something, you have to set it free.

The Days of Summer

Eve Bunting, Author

William Low, Illustrator

Harcourt, 2001

How could this be happening? Grandparents aren't supposed to get divorced. As Nora and Jo-Jo struggle to find ways to bring them back together, they find that love can make even the most terrible of situations bearable. As always, Bunting has taken a contemporary issue and turned it into a gentle but honest tale of real life and how it doesn't always have a happy ending. She deals with the process of acceptance and growth.

A Day's Work

Eve Bunting, Author

Ronald Himler, Illustrator

Clarion, 1994

What is the price of a lie? Young Francisco and his grandfather are looking for a day's work. When a man offers them a gardening job, they agree, even though the grandfather's trade is carpentry. The lure of cash overpowers his good judgment, and the two begin to weed the garden. Imagine their surprise when they realize they have weeded out the *flowers*. The grandfather is ashamed and teaches his grandson an important lesson in integrity when he insists on returning the next day to remedy the problem. In return, the employer realizes that Francisco and his grandfather are fine workers whom he is happy to employ again over time. This poignant story is a powerful platform for discussions about ideas on personal character and work ethic.

So Far From the Sea

Eve Bunting, Author

Chris K. Soentpiet, Illustrator

Clarion, 1998

Tender and culturally sensitive, this work takes us back to the days of the U.S. Japanese internment camps during World War II. Young authors will appreciate the historical information and the literary technique of "back story," telling much of the story through the father's eyes from years' past. *So Far From the Sea* is a book to be studied not only for its messages, but also for its craft.

Trouble on the T-Ball Team

Eve Bunting, Author

Irene Trivas, Illustrators

Clarion Books, 1997

Who doesn't love a surprise—especially a reader? Eve Bunting uses a baseball game as the backdrop for this piece. Linda has lost something and from all accounts, it's something important. As the baseball game unfolds, we get little hints of what it is. Finally, as the game ends, we find out what was lost. The timing is perfect, both on the field and for Linda. Giving little hints throughout, using small moments to make big points—Eve Bunting does this beautifully and creates a model for writers to try in their own stories.

Players in Pigtails

Shana Corey, Author

Rebecca Gibson, Illustrator

Scholastic, 2003

There are quite a few books about women in baseball, but this one is my favorite. It's lively and filled with interesting facts. For example, did you know that the song "Take Me Out to the Ball Game" was written for a girl? I sure didn't. This book is an excellent example of how to write about historical information and make it personal and fascinating to the reader.

A Fine, Fine School

Sharon Creech, Author

Harry Bliss, Illustrator

HarperCollins, 2001

Sharon Creech is one of my favorite authors of books for children and young adults, but with this picture book she writes for all of us. *A Fine, Fine School* is the story of a school where the principal keeps adding time to the school week until there are no breaks or weekends. The students and teachers realize that their school isn't so fine anymore. Learning stops until the principal realizes that much of what is important in life is learned outside of school—not just in school. Students will have a great time reading and reacting to this book. Invite them to consider the idea of how much school is too much. I'm sure they will give you ideas filled with voice!

Weslandia

Paul Fleischman, Author

Kevin Hawkes, Illustrator

Candlewick Press, 1999

Finding a good idea is one of the hardest parts of writing and this book will show students one way to find an interesting topic for writing. Wesley is one of those kids who doesn't like to do things the way other children do. When confronted with a long summer vacation, he comes up with a brilliant idea of how to spend his time. "Suddenly, Wesley's thoughts shot sparks. His eyes blazed. His father was right! He could actually *use* what he'd learned that week for a summer project that would top all the others. He could grow his own staple food crop—and found his own civilization." From that idea comes a story that will keep students and adults turning the pages!

Out of the Ocean

Debra Frasier, Author and Illustrator

Harcourt, 1998

It's those little moments that inspire the best ideas for writing. Here, Debra Frasier takes us into one of those moments, a quiet walk on the beach. She paints a picture in your mind. Her text is so real, so right, that you can smell the salt air and feel the sand between your toes. This work is a perfect study for how to write about small things so they really resonate with the reader.

Roller Coaster

Marla Frazee, Author and Illustrator

Harcourt, 2003

Take a small moment, blow it up, and relive it from all of its many interesting angles. That's the way this action-packed piece on roller coasters unfolds. Some writers think they have to write about the whole day or every attraction at the amusement part. Not Marla Frazee. She gives us one moment in time on one ride so clearly that we feel we are experiencing it right along with the characters in the story.

Lilly's Purple Plastic Purse

Kevin Henkes, Author and Illustrator

Greenwillow Books, 1996

With a title like this, how can you miss? This charming book is full of virtuoso voice and wonderful word choice. What really sells this book, however, is the clever idea. When Lilly gets a brand new purple plastic purse and glittery movie star sunglasses, she can't wait to show them to her classmates. The problem is, she shows them when her teacher is trying to teach. Needless to say, the teacher is unhappy about being interrupted. In a rich, lighthearted way, Henkes shows us how Lilly learns to deal with her anger toward her teacher. See focus lesson on page 28.

Faraway Home

Jane Kurtz, Author

Earl B. Lewis, Illustrator

Harcourt, 2000

Authors of books for children and adults frequently visit the concept of home. In this particularly fine book, Jane Kurtz gives us two different perspectives on home in one family. Desta's father yearns to return to his home, Ethiopia, while Desta thinks of America as her home because it's the only one she has ever known. As the father and daughter come into conflict over what matters most to them, readers of all ages will appreciate this poignant exploration of the true meaning of home.

Before I Was Your Mother

Kathryn Lasky, Author

LeUyen Pham, Illustrator

Harcourt, 2003

We've all heard the stories from our parents about what life was like in the "olden days." In this lovely work by noted author Kathryn Lasky, a mother and daughter share the stories and the memories of what the mother's life was like before she was a mom. This piece is filled with specific details and gives us a glimpse into the mother's past and, perhaps, our own. "I wasn't always your mother, who carries a purse full of bills to pay and wears shoes that won't hurt my feet. Once I was a little girl, who carried secret stuff in a green velvet bag and wanted a pair of bright red patent-leather shoes more than anything." It is a magnificent example of how to use details, lots of them, to create something quite big and important.

Reptiles Are My Life

Megan McDonald, Author

Paul Brett Johnson, Illustrator

Scholastic, 2001

Books that mix fact and fiction provide good models for writing about factual information in different formats. This text is a great example of just that—a good story combined with all sorts of interesting bits of information about reptiles. It's funny and true to life at the same time—the perfect book to study to learn how to blend genres.

The Honest-to-Goodness Truth

Patricia C. McKissack, Author

Giselle Potter, Illustrator

Aladdin Paperbacks, Simon & Schuster, 2000

Taking a big idea and breaking it down into a series of smaller ones is an art. In this story, young Libby learns that telling the truth is always the way to go. But she also learns that telling the truth can be hurtful. Through a series of episodes, Libby learns that how you tell the truth can make all the difference and that keeping other people's feelings in mind as you tell them what they need to know is important. Students learn to write about an important topic like honesty. McKissack uses relevant stories and anecdotes to peel off the layers of a complex subject to the core level where it really works for readers.

Rose's Journal: The Story of a Girl in the Great Depression

Marissa Moss, Author and Illustrator

Harcourt, 2001

This book is part of a series that I like very much. Each book has a lot of information, but because the format utilizes handwritten text and hand-drawn illustrations, the idea of approaching a research project this way seems manageable and within the grasp of most young writers. If you like to collect books and resources around themes, this book would be a nice addition for the Great Depression, coupled with a longer work such as Karen Hesse's *Out of the Dust*. Students could read and compare their impressions of what life was like during this historic time from the point of view of the two female narrators.

Aaron's Hair

Robert Munsch, Author

Alan Daniel, Illustrator

Scholastic, 2000

Take a simple idea like having a head of unmanageable hair and turn it into a story. That's quite a challenge for most of us, but Robert Munsch has done a magnificent job of showing us that the best stories are those that focus on a small topic but use lots of specific details. After sharing this piece with students, ask them to think of little things about themselves that they don't like (such as hair color, size of feet, height, or color of eyes) and create similar pieces using Munsch's techniques. If you break the story down into pieces, it will be relatively easy to replicate.

Stone Soup

Jon J. Muth, Author and Illustrator

Scholastic, 2003

In Muth's text, this famous story is retold in the Chinese tradition. As villagers join together to make stone soup, they learn about each other, how to trust each other, and how to celebrate each other. There are many different versions of this story, from many different cultural perspectives. Its message is timeless. Its idea is powerful.

The Three Questions

Jon J. Muth, Author and Illustrator

Scholastic, 2002

Based on writings by Leo Tolstoy, this elegant picture book is certain to promote thoughtful discussions about values. When is the best time to do things? Who is the most important one? What is the right thing to do? These three questions are posed and answered in a moving fable that students of all ages will enjoy. See focus lesson on page 31.

Wings

Christopher Myers, Author and Illustrator

Scholastic, 2000

We ask students to find topics that matter to them and write, which, I admit, is much easier said than done. It's particularly hard when students feel that if they write about what is meaningful to them, other students may ridicule them. In this powerful piece, Christopher Myers allows readers to feel empathy with the main character as they read about Ikarus Jackson, a boy who knows how to fly. By flapping his wings as he gets ready to soar, Ikarus is encouraged to be different and let his own, unique spirit take wing.

Bikes for Rent!

Isaac Olaleye, Author

Chris L. Demarest, Illustrator

Orchard Books, 2001

Set in western Nigeria, this delightful story takes us back to our own childhood when we desperately wanted something, but couldn't afford it. Lateef wants a bike. So he works and works and finally earns enough money to rent one. While riding, Lateef crashes and has to figure out a way to pay for the bike, even though it isn't his own. There's an awfully nice character message to discuss and write about from this story: Should children have to work for what they want?

Thank You, Mr. Falker

Patricia Polacco, Author and Illustrator

Philomel Books, 1998

Imagine a book that is beautifully written, has an important message for all students and adults, *and* is a tribute to teachers. Now add in that the story is based on the author's real life, and you'll understand why you'll need a tissue handy for this one. This story centers on one eager young student who can't figure out letters and numbers until a gifted teacher steps in and helps make it all work for her. Patricia Polacco writes to make us feel deeply about important topics and this time she strikes an arrow right into the heart of teaching and shows the difference one person who cares can make in the life of a child.

The Hickory Chair

Lisa Rowe Fraustino, Author

Benny Andrews, Illustrator

Scholastic, 2001

This is a love story; a tale of the deep and abiding love between a grandmother and her grandson. Gran tells wonderful stories to Louis and, even though he is blind, he believes he can see and feel all the sights and people she describes. When Gran dies, it seems that she has remembered everyone in the notes she left scattered about the house—except for Louis. Louis is lost and must search for his sense of self without her. In this incredibly brilliant text, the reader will gain an appreciation of the bond between grandparent and grandchild and be reminded of the awesome power of love. See focus lesson on page 32.

Home to Medicine Mountain

Chiori Santiago, Author

Judith Lowry, Illustrator

Children's Book Press, 1998

Attention to the little details is one of the many fine qualities you will notice in this picture book. It is the story of two young brothers who are separated from their family and sent to live at a government-run Indian residential school in the 1930s—an experience all too common for young Native American children of the time. As you read, notice the details that make the story so real: the shoes on the feet of the boarding school's headmaster, the stiffness of the school uniforms, the harshness of the school day. In such a short text, the reader gets caught up in how it felt to be yanked from your family and forced to live in a whole new way, one that is completely foreign and so very, very lonely.

Nothing Ever Happens on 90th Street

Roni Schotter, Author

Krysten Brooker, Illustrator

Orchard Books, 1997

Go on an adventure with the young author in this lively book. Convinced that she has nothing to write about, young Eva works her way through the neighborhood looking for something interesting to put in her composition. Not too surprisingly to us, but quite a shock to Eva, she finds out that some pretty amazing things are happening right under her nose! See focus lesson on page 13.

A Bad Case of Stripes

David Shannon, Author and Illustrator

Kathleen Westray, Illustrator

Scholastic, 1998

Camilla Cream loves lima beans but she pretends she doesn't so other kids won't make fun of her. Camilla discovers how important it is to be true to yourself, to be an individual, when she comes down with a bad case of stripes and finds her skin has turned shades of the brightest colors. It seems the only thing to cure it is to admit that she loves lima beans. Students who need a little reminder about how special they are just for being themselves—lima beans and all—will enjoy reading this piece and writing about their own likes and dislikes.

Antarctic Antics: A Book of Penguin Poems

Judy Sierra, Author

Ariane Dewey, Illustrator

Harcourt, 1998

Take a delightful dive into the world of penguins in this collection of witty poems. From eating habits to mating habits, this book covers a lot of ground. If students are confused about how to take facts and turn them into interesting text filled with surprises, this book will be an excellent example of how one author does it well. Encourage students to select their own animals or other real-life topics and use this book's poems as models to write their own collections.

Through the Cracks

Carolyn Sollman, Barbara Emmons, and Judith Paolini, Authors

Sterling Publishing, 1994

Through the Cracks is a cleverly illustrated story about how dismal a school can be when it doesn't work. Told through the eyes of one student—literally shrunk to the size where she can fall "through the cracks" of the school floor—it reminds us all that schools should be places where the needs of students come first, where activities are stimulating, and where learning is celebrated. See focus lesson on page 9.

How I Spent My Summer Vacation

Mark Teague, Author and Illustrator

Dragonfly Books, 1995

In this delightful twist on the old "summer vacation" paper, Mark Teague takes us on a ride through the Wild West and on a vacation that is more unusual than usual. Filled with descriptive details that make readers feel as if they're traveling right alongside Teague, this book shows us and doesn't just tell us what happens on the journey. It is good inspiration for students to write their own fanciful stories about their summer vacations.

I Spy: Extreme Challenger!

Jean Marzollo, Author

Walter Wick, Illustrator/Photographer

Scholastic, 2000

The latest in the series of *I Spy* books really takes the prize. Children and adults will be fascinated by the complex photographs and challenging riddles that make them want to dive in and find the hidden objects. Becoming aware of little details that someone else might not notice is one of the keys to success in writing ideas clearly. Surely having this book and the others in the series will help student writers sharpen their descriptive powers—and have a blast along the way!

Fox

Margaret Wild, Author

Ron Brooks, Illustrator

Kane/Miller Publishers, 2001

This book haunts me. I read it, put it down, then pick it up and read it again—unsure whether I read it correctly. Then I call someone and read it to her so I can talk about the ideas, the symbolism, the many layers of meaning. Finally, I ask myself, "Who is screaming at the end? Fox? Dog?" This is a book for older readers and writers and is certainly something to talk about at length. Trust me—this is a book that is quite unusual and spectacular.

The Secret Knowledge of Grown-Ups

David Wisniewski, Author and Illustrator

Lothrop, Lee & Shepard, 1998

You know all the rules we were told as children and have passed along to our children, such as "Eat your vegetables" and "Comb your hair"? Wisniewski has cleverly brought them to life by giving the real, untold reasons behind these rules. Told in a most lively and engaging style, with graphics to die for, this piece can be used as a writing prompt for exploring other rules and commonly held perceptions. Let your students brainstorm their own experiences. Then divide them into groups to see who can come up with the most original and fantastic ideas for writing. See focus lesson on page 27.

The Secret Knowledge of Grown-Ups: The Second File

David Wisniewski, Author and Illustrator

HarperCollins, 2001

Thank goodness there is a second book in this series. Each "secret" has its own solution. Use this book as a model for students as they learn to look past the obvious and come up with new ideas for creating their own "secret files." On a sad note, David Wisniewski died in 2002. He will be missed by those of us who admire his work, enjoy his art, and appreciate his outstanding contribution to children's literature.

A Quiet Place

Douglas Wood, Author

Dan Andreasen, Illustrator

Simon and Schuster, 2002

The world is so fast-paced and hectic that finding a quiet place can be a challenge. This lovely book invites us to find that place within ourselves, where the world slows down, where the silence feels good, and where we get in touch with what really matters. In describing places where many people go to find quiet, the author uses wonderful details and visual images to create pictures in our minds. This book will remind you how important it is to take a deep breath every now and again. See focus lesson on page 30.

Seven Blind Mice

Ed Young, Author and Illustrator

Philomel Books, 1992

The central message of this book sums up the most important message of the writing classroom: "Knowing in part may make a fine tale, but wisdom comes from seeing the whole." The traits are a piece of this whole. Use them to empower your students to make writing a joyous part of their lives.

Focus Lessons for Inspiring Ideas

Focus Lesson Based On . . .

The Secret Knowledge of Grown-Ups
David Wisniewski, Author and Illustrator
Lothrop, Lee & Shepard, 1998
(See description page 26.)

Target Trait: Ideas
Secondary Traits: Organization, Voice

Learning to see the world with humor, energy, and imagination is the lesson of this book. As students read, they will appreciate Wisniewski's ability to explain all the "secret" rules that grown-ups have and don't tell children. In this lesson, students work to write their own secret rules—a wonderful exercise for developing creative ideas.

Materials:

- A copy of *The Secret Knowledge of Grown-Ups*
- Overhead transparencies and markers
- Writing paper and pens or pencils

What to Do:

1. Read *The Secret Knowledge of Grown-Ups* to the class and discuss the key ideas that the author uses to intrigue the reader.
2. Review the trait of ideas with students, showing why the author would score high.
3. Have a class discussion about "secret rules" that most kids have to follow, such as eating their vegetables and combing their hair. Then choose one or two of these rules that small groups or pairs can write about on their own.
4. Discuss the voice that they think will work best. Explore the differences between a kid's voice in writing and an adult's voice.

5. Look at the patterns of organization in *The Secret Knowledge of Grown-Ups* and help students decide on an organization to fit their "secret rule" idea.

6. Allow plenty of time for students to write and illustrate using markers, paints, magazine cutouts, and so on. Be sure to plan time to share the final stories.

Follow Up:

- Create collections of "secret rules" books and share them with other classes.
- Have students use their writer's notebooks to keep a running list of possible new rules for future writing topics.

Focus Lesson Based On . . .

Lilly's Purple Plastic Purse

Kevin Henkes

Greenwillow Books, 1996

(See description on page 19.)

Target Trait: Ideas

Secondary Traits: Voice, Word Choice

This book is a wonderful study in characters—who they are, how they develop, and what matters to them. So for this lesson, students work with the trait of ideas by identifying details about characters. They create their own character, create a problem for him or her to solve, and write a short story draft. Henkes's charming book also works well for the trait of voice. The characters are familiar and have to deal with issues that most students can relate to. Henke writes with authenticity and allows readers to relate to the ideas on a personal level.

Materials:

- A copy of *Lilly's Purple Plastic Purse*
- Overhead transparencies and markers
- Writing paper and pens or pencils

WHAT TO DO:

1. Talk to students about why it's important to use descriptive details in writing. Read a passage from a book that your class has enjoyed and that contains good details—pick a wonderful book. Ask students to list all the details in their notebooks or by calling out details while you list them on the overhead.

2. Expand the discussion by asking the class to talk about different characters and people they know. Categorize them: friends, family, school buddies, other significant adults, and so forth.

3. Ask students to pick one of these groups and write down details about the kinds of problems people in the group encounter, such as dealing with sibling rivalry, standing up to bullies, and knowing how to make new friends.

4. Read *Lilly's Purple Plastic Purse* to the class.

5. Discuss Lilly's problems and how she solves them. Have students compare how Lilly handles her problems to how their chosen groups solve their problems. Are there things Lilly could have done differently? Are there things Lilly did to solve her problem that the group does to solve its problem?

6. Have students think of a person, real or imagined. Ask them to draw a picture of that person and write out his or her problem, paying close attention to the details that will make this person more real and believable. For students who do not want to draw, allow them to cut out pictures from magazines.

7. Have students write a short story based on their illustrations, focusing on the character's problem and how he or she might solve it. Remind students to use good, detailed descriptions, as Kevin Henkes does.

8. Share the stories and illustrations and discuss the important role of character details.

FOLLOW UP:

- Have students rewrite and revise their stories with the intent of publishing.
- Create a public place—bulletin board, library display area, a table in the entryway of the school lobby—where the stories and illustrations can be displayed.

Focus Lesson Based On . . .

A Quiet Place
Douglas Wood, Author
Dan Andreasen, Illustrator
Simon and Schuster, 2002
(See description on page 26.)

Target Trait: Ideas
Secondary Traits: Word Choice, Voice

As students work with the trait of ideas, they learn that the best ideas are those that are focused. Being able to get inside a small idea and make it big is part of what this lesson teaches. It encourages students to look at the ordinary in new and imaginative ways.

Materials:

- A copy of A *Quiet Place*
- Overhead transparencies and markers
- Writing papers and pens or pencils
- Digital or traditional cameras (optional)

What to Do:

1. As a class, generate a list of noisy places, such as the school cafeteria, a city street, a concert, an airport, and a construction site. Record them on the overhead transparency.

2. Ask, "Where do you go when you want to get away from noise? Where are quiet places?" Record ideas.

3. Read A *Quiet Place* aloud.

4. Prepare to go on a "quiet hunt." Have small groups of students generate lists of places they could capture in words (or pictures, if cameras are available), on school grounds or in the community.

5. Send students out of the classroom to capture the quiet places they find. If they go beyond school grounds, be sure they have supervision. When students return, have

them write descriptions of their quiet places and include photos or drawings on the final copy.

6. Create a book of the quiet places students found.

Follow Up:

- Ask students to find another quiet place to describe and photograph. Create a collection of quiet places to put into a book for all students to look at and enjoy. Encourage students to write reflective pieces on the value of having some quiet time in their lives every day. Add their pieces to this collection.
- Brainstorm with students what the ideal quiet place at home looks like. Ask them to draw pictures of their imagined quiet places at home and describe them in detail.

Focus Lesson Based On . . .

The Three Questions

Jon J. Muth, Author and Illustrator

Scholastic, 2002

(See description on page 22.)

Target Trait: Ideas

Secondary Trait: Organization

This lesson gives students the opportunity to work from big ideas to narrower, more focused ones. Working from Leo Tolstoy's original idea, students have the opportunity to write multiple times, trying to find a central point to answer each of the three questions from the story.

Materials:

- A copy of *The Three Questions*
- Small index cards, three per student
- Writing paper and pens or pencils

What to Do:

1. Give each student three index cards and ask them to label each at the top with these three questions: When is the best time to do things? Who is the most important one? What is the right thing to do?

2. Allow time for students to write a one- to two-sentence answer to each question on the cards. Have them draw a line under their answer. For example, When is the best time to do things? A student might write, "In the morning when you are fresh." Or, "Right away when you are thinking about it so you don't forget." Share responses as a class and discuss.

3. Read *The Three Questions* and stop after page six, which reads, "'Fighting,' barked Pushkin right away."

4. Ask students to write more about each question on the front of the card. This time when they write, you can expect to see the answers to the questions become more thoughtful and more focused on a big idea. The first time through, students write quite literally, specifically, and sometimes superficially, but as they think about the ideas in the story they get a chance to write at a deeper level, showing how their thinking gets right to the heart of the main idea.

5. Finish reading *The Three Questions*. Direct students to use the backs of their index cards to write their reaction to Muth's answer for each question. Ask students to write about any surprises they discovered in Muth's answers. Or, they can compare Muth's answer to each question to their own. Discuss.

Follow Up:

- Have students create skits from their new stories demonstrating the importance of the three questions in everyday life at school.
- Read Tolstoy's original short story, "The Three Questions," and explore the way Muth changed the characters and details, yet maintained the original theme.

Focus Lesson Based On . . .

The Hickory Chair

Lisa Rowe Fraustino, Author
Benny Andrews, Illustrator
Scholastic, 2001
(See description on page 23.)

Target Trait: Ideas
Secondary Traits: Word Choice, Voice

Finding worthwhile topics for writing is a hard job for many students. This lesson shows how a topic can come from a simple, everyday thing. In Rowe Fraustino's story, that thing is a hickory chair, which works as a symbol of a loving grandparent/grandchild relationship.

MATERIALS:

- A copy of *The Hickory Chair*
- Overhead transparency and markers
- Writing paper and pens or pencils

WHAT TO DO:

1. Ask the students if they think they could write a whole story about a chair. Brainstorm what a writer would need to know about a chair to make it the centerpiece for a story. For example: What is it made of? How old is it? Who sits in it? Has anyone else ever owned this chair? Are there any marks on the chair? Record the ideas for students to look at later.

2. Remind students that good writers usually anticipate and answer the readers' questions in order to make their ideas clear.

3. Read *The Hickory Chair* aloud.

4. Return to the list of student-generated questions about the chair. Were they all answered in this story? If not, ask students, "Why do you suppose the author didn't include that particular information?" Discuss how authors pick and choose pieces of information to include in their writing to make the central idea clear and focused—and not cluttered.

5. Ask students, "What is the main idea of this piece? Is it really about a chair?" Discuss how a symbol can stand for a bigger idea in a story. In this case, the hickory chair becomes a symbol for the love between the grandmother and her grandson.

6. In small groups, direct students to think about special objects that they have that are symbols for friendships, special relationships, and treasured memories of special events.

7. Using these objects as the focus of a new piece of writing, ask students to make a list of questions about their object that they think should be answered. Have them share these questions with the group.

8. Direct the students to write a story or essay that features this object in a way that the reader will see it as a symbol of something important.

Chapter Two

Shaping Organization

"The texts children write are more likely to resemble the texts of picture books than longer books composed of extended chapters. Whatever their reading preference, [children in second grade and beyond] will need the picture books as models for their writing."

—Thomas Newkirk
Beyond Words: Picture Books for Older Readers and Writers

Picture books can give students ideas for organizing their work. As they examine these texts, encourage students to look for ways authors begin and end their pieces. Examine texts for how the authors use transitions, sequence words, and move readers smoothly through the book. Another organizational element to watch for is pacing. Have students notice how much information the author gives out and how quickly. Students will be amazed to discover how authors zoom in to spend more time in a few key places, then fast forward to the next important idea.

Organization is a challenge for any writer. Picture books give us a wonderful place to examine how authors craft text to keep ideas flowing at just the right rate.

Organization: A Definition

Organization is the internal structure of a piece of writing, the thread of central meaning, the pattern of logic. Structure can be based on comparison-contrast, deductive logic, point-by-point analysis, development of a central theme, chronological play of events, or any of a dozen other identifiable patterns. A piece with strong organization begins with a clear purpose that creates anticipation in the reader. Events proceed logically. Information is given to the reader in the right doses at the right times so that the reader never loses the "big picture"—the overriding sense of what the writer is driving at. Connections between ideas are strong, which is another way of saying that the bridges from one idea to the next hold up. The piece closes with a sense of resolution, tying up loose ends, bringing things to closure, answering important questions while still leaving the reader something to wonder and think about.

Lin Steele, a fourth-grade teacher, noticed that her students were having difficulty with paragraph structure—knowing where to indent and start a new paragraph—because the idea had shifted. So she browsed her bookshelf and came up with the perfect "micro text" (a picture book that has complex text on each page, sophisticated story lines, and risky presentation) and a wonderful lesson, which, according to Lin, "worked like a dream. I couldn't believe how well they did! The incredible thing about this story was how some of the students who haven't really 'gotten into' the writing process seemed to really tie in to the map. There wasn't a single student who didn't produce on this assignment."

Feature Focus Lesson Based On . . .

The Secret Shortcut

Mark Teague, Author and Illustrator

Scholastic, 1996

(See description on page 48.)

Target Trait: Organization

Secondary Trait: Conventions

Wendell and Floyd are prone to telling some pretty tall tales about why they are late to school. Aliens, pirates, and a plague of frogs are excuses tried but discarded because their teacher doesn't believe them one little bit. The boys decide to reform their bad habit and to get to school on time, so they take a shortcut. This turns out to be quite the adventure as a whole new series of stumbling blocks arise that challenge their goal of punctuality. In this lesson students design their own "shortcuts" to school as they examine the organization of Mark Teague's text as a model.

Materials:

- A copy of *The Secret Shortcut*
- Chart paper
- Drawing/construction paper
- Markers
- Writing paper and pens or pencils

What to Do:

Day 1

1. Read *The Secret Shortcut* aloud.

2. Discuss and list on chart paper all the things that happen to Wendell and Floyd on the way to school. Hang the list in a prominent place so all students can see and refer to it.

3. Give each group of two to three students a large piece of construction paper and have them draw a map creating a brand new shortcut to school for the main characters. Encourage students to be creative about things they might encounter along the way, such as volcanoes, bottomless pits, quicksand, and so forth, expanding on ideas from the original story.

Day 2

1. Discuss the student-created map as a prewriting activity.

2. Create new "Secret Shortcuts" stories in small groups. Use a sentence starter like: "Wendell and Floyd took a new shortcut to school," if you wish.

3. Discuss the sequencing words that can help organize the events of the story.

Sequencing words and phrases

before, after, then, next, during, finally, sometimes, often, first, second, third, earlier, later, now, last, at first, first of all, to begin with, in the first place, at the same time, for now, for the time being, the next step, in time, in turn, later on, meanwhile, soon, in the meantime, while, simultaneously, afterward

4. Have students write at least three detailed sentences to describe each event on the map.

5. Tell students to start a paragraph each time there is a new sequencing word that leads to a different event. For example, if the map shows a bottomless pit, they might begin a paragraph this way: "*After* reaching the bottomless pit, Wendell and Floyd tiptoed around the edges, trying frantically not to fall in. The pit was dark, shadowy, and seemed as though it was reaching out to grab them as they tried to sneak by."

FOLLOW UP:

- Find examples of sequencing words in other texts and talk about how they link ideas.
- Help students make a chart with the words and sentences showing how to use them. Hang it in the classroom. Look through other picture books to find strong and obvious organizational patterns that really work. Here are a few to get you started.

Picture Books for Shaping Organization

The Magic Fan

Keith Baker, Author and Illustrator

Voyager Books, 1984

Richly illustrated with a detailed Japanese fan, this text is a classic piece that students will want to return to over and over again. Baker's attention to detail and his use of a fold-out fan on every page makes the book enjoyable to readers of all ages. You see the clear development of a story, with all of its key elements, and some excellent examples of sequencing and transition words throughout.

When Sophie Gets Angry—Really, Really Angry . . .

Molly Bang, Author and Illustrator

Scholastic, 1999

As always, Bang hits a home run with this compassionate and affirming work. We do all get angry sometimes, and what do we do about it? In *When Sophie Gets Angry*, we learn many different ways to work through our feelings. The book is organized into problem/solution scenarios. And, most wonderfully, the ending takes us to a place where we want to be, a house that "is warm and smells good."

Three Cheers for Catherine the Great!

Cari Best, Author

Giselle Potter, Illustrator

DK Publishing, 1999

Sara, a young Russian girl, is surprised and perplexed when Grandma Ekaterina (a.k.a. Catherine) announces that she doesn't want anyone to buy birthday presents for her. What? No presents for Grandma? How can that be? Sara thinks back in time to all the events of her grandmother's life, searching for a present she can give her without spending any money. Others in the family follow suit, but Sara turns out to be the most resourceful, delighting her grandmother with the most special gift of all. Best and Potter use the idea of *no presents* to show Catherine's early life in Russia, her later life in America, and her transition between lives. This piece is a marvel of sequencing, and, like so many other picture books, has a marvelous ending—simple yet perfect. See focus lesson on page 50.

Switch on the Night

Ray Bradbury, Author

Leo and Diane Dillon, Illustrators

Alfred A. Knopf, 1993

The one and only picture book by one of my favorite authors, Ray Bradbury, this piece is timeless. An unreasonable fear of the dark is common to many of us, and Bradbury tackles it in a beautifully written fable. The imagination, originality, and brilliance of this piece make it a "must have." The organization is sophisticated and lends itself to many different teaching approaches. You could look at repeating refrains and note how this helps give emphasis to the main idea. You could make a story map of events and how they build to a resolution. You could compare and contrast the beginning and the ending, and discuss their similarities and differences. *Switch on the Night* has endless possibilities for study. But first and foremost, read it and enjoy its message. I think it was written for children, but certainly for the child in all of us.

Through My Eyes

Ruby Bridges, Author

Scholastic, 1999

I take this book everywhere. By using stories, poems, time lines, quotations, observations, photographs, and many other source materials, Bridges organizes the material so we understand the historic impact of a six-year-old black child who courageously breaks the color barrier of her time. A whole unit on civil rights could be built around this book—regardless of the grade level. I applaud the author and the editors for putting such a fine piece of American history into the hands of children and adults. See focus lesson on page 56.

Butterfly House

Eve Bunting, Author

Greg Shed, Illustrator

Scholastic, 1999

Enough is enough, Eve. Don't you ever write bad books? Each new piece you share with us explores new feelings, tackles new issues, and inspires. You are truly remarkable. In *Butterfly House*, we learn about the many stages in the life cycle of the caterpillar. From the transformation from caterpillar larva to chrysalis to butterfly, we watch and learn. The passage of time underscores the movement of the piece. Carefully and beautifully organized, we are moved to a new understanding of this remarkable creature. This book is an excellent example of the organization being so strong that it silently sweeps you up and lets you enjoy the unique treatment of the topic.

Click, Clack, Moo: Cows That Type

Doreen Cronin, Author

Betsy Lewin, Illustrator

Simon and Schuster, 2000

Stories need problems to be solved. In this uproarious piece, Farmer Brown has a problem, all right. He has cows that type and keep sending him messages about ways to make them more comfortable. It starts with electric blankets and goes on from there. These literate cows turn Farmer Brown's life upside down as a series of letters between the farmer and the cows sets up a back-and-forth organizational structure to move the story forward. Adults will appreciate the subtleties that parallel our working lives. See focus lesson on page 54.

Grandpa Never Lies

Ralph Fletcher, Author

Harvey Stevenson, Illustrator

Clarion Books, 2000

In this endearing story rooted in Fletcher's childhood, the repeating refrain "Grandpa never lies" is used to move the reader along. The precious relationship between a grandfather and his grandson will touch your heart. You'll find yourself looking forward to and anticipating every adventure, every anecdote, every explanation of even the most common of things, all of which are punctuated by that grand line, "Grandpa never lies." It will make you remember; it will make you smile. This is an excellent book for sentence fluency and voice, also.

Circle of Thanks

Susi Gregg Fowler, Author

Peter Catalanotto, Illustrator

Scholastic, 1998

The changing of the seasons is the organizational device here. Fowler captures life on the Alaskan tundra through the cycle of a full year. She paints an indelible picture in the minds of readers, who will appreciate how this story is laid out to mirror the changing colors and textures of this amazing place. As a fan of watercolor, I really appreciate the soft, yet incredibly detailed illustrations.

Chief

Chris Ganci, Author

Scholastic, 2003

This is a loving tribute to Chris Ganci's father, a New York City firefighter who was lost that terrible day in September 2001, organized around themes related to his father's career, from his training ("Firefighter"), to his high point ("A Good Job"), to his untimely death ("Goodbye"). This book teaches readers what it is like to be a firefighter by focusing on one remarkable man. Students who have a hard time understanding how longer text can be interesting and can support illustrations will appreciate the organization, the ideas, and the voice of this fine book.

The Good Luck Cat

Joy Harjo, Author

Paul Lee, Illustrator

Harcourt, 2000

For anyone who has truly loved a pet, this book is for you. The stories are organized to show how Woogie the cat lost each of her nine lives. Tucked between a brilliant introduction and heartwarming conclusion is a story organized around a true idea, not a prescribed number of paragraphs. You will want to use this book for word choice, too. Listen to the beautiful language in the opening paragraph: "I have a cat, a stripedy cat with tickling whiskers and green electric eyes. She has the softest fur in the world. When I pet her she purrs as if she has a drum near her heart." I love this book, and, honest, not because one of my cats looks exactly like Woogie!

Rocks in His Head

Carol Otis Hurst, Author

James Stevenson, Illustrator

Greenwillow Books, 2001

Using the line "You've got rocks in your head" throughout, this piece documents how a man's love for rocks leads him to the job of his dreams during the Depression. It shows us what following a passion can do for us. This is a gentle, quiet, and compassionate book. Hurst uses the typically negative refrain that the author's father heard all his life as the organizer and spins it into something very positive—a good model for student writers to try on their own.

City by Numbers

Stephen T. Johnson, Author and Illustrator

Penguin Putnam, 1998

A perfect companion to Stephen Johnson's other picture book masterpiece, *Alphabet City*, this book challenges us to look closely at our surroundings for numbers. When a writer looks closely to see the details others might miss, we say he or she is working with the ideas trait. That is certainly true for this book, but the way it is organized is worth studying, too. Ask students to find numbers around the school, on the playground, or at home. Then have them bring those numbers back to class and create new texts organized like Johnson's. See focus lesson on page 53.

Charlie's Checklist

Rory S. Lerman, Author

Alison Bartlett, Illustrator

Orchard Books, 1997

Charlie is a dog looking for a good home, so he puts an ad in the newspaper. When piles of letters come pouring in, Charlie decides that he needs to organize the letters using criteria to pinpoint what he is looking for in a new owner. After reading stacks and stacks of letters and applying his criteria, Charlie realizes that he's known the perfect owner all along. This is a marvelous book for students who are just learning about the traits because it will help them understand the importance of using criteria to make decisions.

Stand Tall, Molly Lou Melon

Patty Lovell, Author

David Catrow, Illustrator

G.P. Putnam's Sons, 2001

Something as simple as the refrain can work wonderfully as the pivotal organizational device in a story. In this sweet piece, it's "And so she did." Molly Lou gets teased by the other children a lot, but her grandmother reminds her at every turn to walk proudly, stand tall, and smile big. And when Molly Lou moves to a new town and school where she doesn't have her grandmother to fall back on, she realizes that she needs to find the strength within herself to be unique and make her own way in her new life. *And so she does.*

Sisters

David McPhail, Author and Illustrator

Harcourt, 2003

Students who read and enjoy this book, a study in comparison and contrast, will also see an example of how to organize their ideas so they really stand out. McPhail starts by focusing on how sisters are different, then moves to how they are alike, giving specific examples all along the way. He dedicates the final page to the most special thing of all that sisters share: love. "But the way they were most alike was the most special way of all. Because, you see, they loved each other so very much." Students who want to write comparison-and-contrast pieces would do well to study the structure of this book.

Plantzilla

Jerdine Nolen, Author

David Catrow, Illustrator

Harcourt, 2002

This is the story of a plant that has a special place in the heart of the teacher as well as the students in this rather remarkable class. Its back-and-forth organizational structure furthers the story while providing many important details of how to care for a plant, telling why plants are important to our atmosphere, and revealing interesting tidbits. This story has some great surprises—one of which is the warm and loving message of friendship.

Raising Dragons

Jerdine Nolen, Author

Elise Primavera, Illustrator

Harcourt, 1998

Teaching students how to write comparison-and-contrast pieces is one way to use this imaginative book. The young protagonist decides to raise a dragon on the farm where he lives with his parents—a farm that is typical in every way. The setting is realistic, the task is imaginative. This book shows all the steps and stages that a young dragon goes through on his way to becoming independent. It is a sweet find that will bring about interesting and informative discussions about organization.

The Journey of Oliver K. Woodman

Darcy Pattison, Author

Joe Cepeda, Illustrator

Harcourt, 2003

In this book, the author uses a postcard exchange to organize the text and keep it flowing. When Uncle Ray is too busy to visit his young niece, Tameka, he sends a life-sized wooden dummy named Oliver K. Woodman across the country to visit her instead. This book is written in postcards from an uncle to his niece and to all the people who help Oliver go from coast to coast. It's a road trip! You'll enjoy this story and maybe even be inspired to create an adventure or two for Oliver on your own, once you share this book with your class.

First Day in Grapes

L. King Pérez, Author

Robert Casilla, Illustrator

Lee & Low Books, 2002

"Chico never could decide if California reminded him of a fruit basket or a pizza." So begins the elegant story of a young boy, the son of migrant farm workers who is *always* the new kid in school because his family is always traveling to find work. Inevitably, Chico has to resolve a major conflict—what to do about the bullies who pick on the newest students. His solution? To stand up for himself and dazzle them with his math skills. This story is a model on all fronts—from beginning to end, with a terrific sense of resolution. Student writers may wish to consider how the line "first day" used repeatedly throughout the text reminds them of first days in their own lives that have presented them with a challenge.

The Paperboy

Dav Pilkey, Author and Illustrator

Orchard Paperbacks, 1999

This is a sweet piece about the early morning routine of a young boy and his dog as they prepare for a paper route. The work flows beautifully from one event to the next—it is elegant in its form and use of subtle transitions, yet brilliant in its simplicity. Share this piece with students and ask them to pay close attention to how Pilkey moves from dark to dawn without hitting the reader over the head with sequence words. I just love this book!

When Lightning Comes in a Jar

Patricia Polacco, Author and Illustrator

Philomel Books, 2002

The chaos of a family reunion and a little girl's first glimpse of fireflies tie this piece together. Polacco works her magic in this intricately organized text that builds to a crescendo as Grandmother tells young Trisha how to catch fireflies in a jar. Each little story is part of the bigger story in this fine text that links one generation to the next through the secret of catching fireflies on a hot summer evening.

The Loudness of Sam

James Proimos, Author and Illustrator

Harcourt, 1999

I'll admit it: I first picked up this book because my son's name is Sam. But once I started reading, I realized that this was quite a find. Richly written and illustrated, it is organized around situations in which young Sam is loud—very loud. At first it seems like Sam is loud just to be loud, but his infectious bravado begins to rub off on other characters in the story, and pretty soon they begin to enjoy life with the same gusto and volume as Sam. By the end, we are treated to a terrific resolution to a potential life problem that is handled with warmth, humor, and lots of smiles.

Little Whistle

Cynthia Rylant, Author

Tim Bowers, Illustrator

Harcourt, 2000

In this first installment of a new series, Rylant takes us on adventures in a neighborhood toy store, after hours, of course. The story is magical and fun, and the author cleverly moves us through the story without relying too heavily on obvious transition words such as *then*, *next*, *after*, and *finally*. It reads smoothly and easily—and that's much easier to do in one's own writing with a good model, like this one.

G Is for Googol: A Math Alphabet Book

David M. Schwartz, Author

Marissa Moss, Illustrator

Tricycle Press, 1998

Could there be a better organizer than the alphabet? I think not. And Schwartz proves it with this detailed, fact-filled book. Beginning with "A is for Abacus," he takes us on a journey of exploration through intriguing math facts and stories. The book is designed to spark the interest of older readers and writers who might find it interesting to go along on this math adventure with the author. *Q Is for Quark: A Science Alphabet Book* is another book by Schwartz to inspire students to use the alphabet format as an organizer for their own research reports.

The Rain Came Down

David Shannon, Author and Illustrator

Scholastic, 2000

The author does a nice job of using cause and effect to organize this imaginative story. It is simple, clear, and right to the point. The illustrations are exaggerated, imaginative, and playful—adding greatly to the depth of the piece. David Shannon has a style all his own, and his books would be interesting to study as a group for an author study. If you live in a rainy area like I do (i.e. Oregon), you'll love this book. If you don't, well, you'll see what you are missing!

The Composition

Antonio Skármeta, Author

Alfonso Ruano, Illustrator

Groundwood Books, 1998

In this powerful little book with a blockbuster conclusion, young Pedro takes some big steps toward fighting the dictatorship that controls his country. The government uses writing as a tool to control its citizens as the schoolchildren unwittingly reveal information about their parents and activities that would get them into all kinds of trouble. Pedro realizes the peril his family is in and writes about imaginary, harmless events, not the real conversations and comings and goings of his loved ones. The book concludes with an incident involving the composition, leaving readers wondering how long this family can live in safety.

Rimshots

Charles R. Smith Jr., Author and Photographer

Penguin Putnam Books, 1999

The subtitle tells it all: basketball pix, rolls, and rhythms. This book is a collection of lists, poems, short essays, stories, and observations about basketball, each written in its own unique style and voice. It is an example of how to organize multiple pieces of writing from different genres into one book on the same theme. Students can use this text as a model for organizing collections of writing on other ideas that matter to them, such as other sports, friends and family, and favorite out-of-school activities.

People

Peter Spier, Author and Illustrator

Doubleday, 1980

This highly acclaimed book illustrates the way people are the same, despite different cultural backgrounds. The author/illustrator organizes the text around these similarities. One example is his discussion of clothes. We all wear them, wanting to look our best—but every region of the world sports different kinds of clothes because of the need to be comfortable in different climates. According to Spier, all people want to be able to record their language. But we are reminded in this text that there are over a hundred different ways to read and write. The book illustrates simple and complex ways humans are alike. I like it for its message, but also for the way it is organized.

The Journey

Sarah Stewart, Author

David Small, Illustrator

Farrar, Straus and Giroux, 2001

Hannah, an Amish girl, leaves her home to visit her Aunt Clara in Chicago. The author organizes this piece to highlight all the discoveries Hannah makes along the way, while remembering her home. The author alternates between entries from Hannah's diary about all the fascinating things she's experiencing in the city and entries in picture form only, which capture the view from her mind's eye of her life back on the farm. It's a fascinating juxtaposition. This piece could be—should be—used in every trait, but it is a standout piece for organization.

Dear Mrs. LaRue: Letters from Obedience School

Mark Teague, Author and Illustrator

Scholastic, 2002

Format, voice, and a very clever idea play out well in this series of letters from Ike LaRue to his Mistress, Mrs. Gertrude R. LaRue. Poor Ike, a dog who was sent to obedience school to learn some manners, anguishes over the rules and all the tricks he must learn. As he grows more and more impatient with the whole adventure, it shows in his letters—until one day when something happens that turns him into the hero he always knew he would be. The point of view of this piece makes it enjoyable to read, and the letter format is clever. You might want to have students write follow-up letters where the story leaves off.

The Secret Shortcut

Mark Teague, Author and Illustrator

Scholastic, 1996

It's hard not to love this book. It's filled with energy and invites the reader to experience the adventures of the characters right along with them, from beginning to end. Nicely organized, this book shows how to use sequence words to move the reader through the story with ease. After students have enjoyed the story and are ready to flex their organizational writing muscles, ask them to write their own stories using the focus lesson on page 36.

The Z Was Zapped

Chris Van Allsburg, Author and Illustrator

Walter Lorraine Books, 1987

Using the alphabet as the organizer, Van Allsburg presents action sentences for each letter to create a story in 26 acts. This clever organizational structure may inspire students to write their own stories in multiple acts using the letters of their names. The excellent use of active verbs is worth noticing and discussing as well.

Courage

Bernard Waber, Author and Illustrator

Houghton Mifflin, 2002

Courage is something we can all use these days—courage to deal with little things like jumping off the high dive, and courage to deal with big things like learning how to say good-bye. Organized around that one simple, yet profound word, this book moves from example to example of courage in action. "Courage is riding your bike the first time without training wheels." "Courage is a blade of grass breaking through the icy snow." Wonderful. And it all comes together in the end with a universal message—"Courage is what we give to each other." I take this book with me as I travel around the country and meet teachers, because teachers are courageous people. I hope this book reminds you of that! See focus lesson on page 51.

A Drop of Water

Walter Wick, Author and Photographer

Scholastic, 1997

Walter Wick's genius photographs will grab any reader's attention. The stunning organization of this book illustrates that the presentation of complex information does not have to be confusing or boring. Wick breaks down all components of water into a page-by-page explanation, inspiring the reader to keep reading and gathering more information as they go. This book is so simply elegant in its design, yet comprehensive; it could be used for almost any grade level.

Sector 7

David Wiesner, Author and Illustrator

Clarion Books, 1999

You can't beat David Wiesner for imagination. His wordless picture books take us to the places of our dreams. All of his works are great, but this one's organization cries out for discussion about whether it works for the reader or not. Without text, the pictures must do all the work—a mighty big task. Ask students to retell this story and make note of all the transitional words they use to link the illustrations. Most likely, they'll be surprised by and proud of how much they already know about organization and what is going on in this story. You'll like this book. It's a bit weird, but you'll never look at a school field trip the same way again.

Jubal's Wish

Audrey Wood, Author

Don Wood, Illustrator

Blue Sky, 2000

In this fanciful tale, we are reminded of the simple pleasures of life. Jubal the frog wants to share the joy of a beautiful day with his friends. But his friends don't want to go along, which presents problem after problem. But Jubal never gives up. The piece works cleverly and creatively to the unexpected ending, which leaves the reader on a higher plane and with a renewed spirit.

Focus Lessons for Shaping Organization

Focus Lesson Based On . . .

Three Cheers for Catherine the Great!
Cari Best, Author
Giselle Potter, Illustrator
DK Publishing, 1999
(See description on page 38.)

Target Trait: Organization
Secondary Traits: Ideas, Voice

After reading this book about life's great gifts, give students a chance to interview their parents, grandparents, siblings, aunts, uncles, cousins, and so forth, and write about their family's history, in chronological order. Students get a chance to gather important family historical events and write them in sequence.

Materials:

- A copy of *Three Cheers for Catherine the Great!*
- Overhead transparencies and markers
- Writing paper and pens or pencils

What to Do:

1. Read *Three Cheers for Catherine the Great!* to students and discuss the events and the sequence words (see chart on page 37) the author uses to keep those events in order.

2. Ask students to select someone in their family and ask him or her one of the following questions:

   When did our family members first come to the United States, and from where? Why did they come? How did family members come to live in the place we now call home? Did they move many times before arriving there? A couple of times? Or have they always lived there? What are the most important events that have happened while family members have lived in this location, or another place they have lived in for several years?

3. Have students take notes at the interview and bring them to class so they can write a family history.

4. Review key sequence words that students will need in their writing pieces: *next, then, finally, first, once, later, after a while*, and so forth. Ask students to write out the history of their family based on their interview notes. Tell them to use the sequencing words to make sure events stay in the order that makes sense.

5. Share family histories and discuss them as a class.

Follow Up:

- Have students write their histories on the computer and illustrate them.
- Make a class book of the family histories to share with all students and their families.

Focus Lesson Based On . . .

Courage

Bernard Waber, Author and Illustrator
Houghton Mifflin, 2002
(See description on page 48.)

Target Trait: Organization
Secondary Trait: Word Choice

The organization of this book centers on the different uses of the word *courage*. So for this lesson, the organization and word choice traits are highly interrelated. As Waber moves from concrete to abstract examples of how courage is displayed in everyday life, the text unfolds. From the simple to the profound, this text expresses many emotions that are evoked with the use of this one word.

Materials:

- A copy of *Courage*
- 2-inch strips of paper cut lengthwise from 11-by-14-inch sheets
- Markers
- Writing paper and pens or pencils

What to Do:

1. Read aloud and discuss *Courage*. Ask students to tell their favorite examples of courage from the text.

2. List those examples on a chart—from serious to lighthearted. Note how each example is unique, yet taken together, the examples give students a broad definition of courage. Select another word such as *freedom*, *honor*, or *justice*.

3. Ask students to brainstorm the different places where that word would apply. For example, *freedom* might be used to describe a benefit of living in a democratic society, or to describe the feeling we all have on the last day of school.

4. Pass out the sentence strips and markers and have students work in pairs to write and, if time allows, illustrate a good example of how the word might be used, such as "Freedom is what you feel when the bell rings on the last day of school." Or, "Freedom is one of the most important principles of American society." Or, "Freedom is what you feel when you kick off a tight pair of shoes after a long day."

5. Post the sentence strips so all students can read them. Ask the students to organize the strips to create a logical flow or pattern.

6. Ask the class to revise any of the sentences that don't work as well as others, paying attention to how clear the example is, how easy it is to read the sentence, and how well the words help the reader create a picture in her or his mind. Add sequence and transitions words between sentences to show connections where desired.

7. Create a picture book like Waber's based on the word and the revised sentence strips.

Follow Up:

- Ask students to look up their word in an unabridged dictionary and discover any new ideas for uses of the word that students may not have thought of yet. Add more pages to their picture book if students wish.
- Look for other picture books in the classroom library collection that use both concrete and abstract examples to help the reader connect with the main ideas. Contrast the organization in one or more of these books to that of *Courage*.

Focus Lesson Based On . . .

City by Numbers

Stephen T. Johnson, Author and Illustrator

Penguin Putnam, 1998

(See description on page 42.)

Target Trait: Organization

Secondary Trait: Ideas

Learning to observe closely is one of the keys to writing success. Using concept books (books that focus on numbers, colors, and letters of the alphabet) can help. Stephen T. Johnson shows students how to look at the world around them and see number shapes—they might see the number 6 in an X or the number 10 in a Y. This book is a nice model for students to follow as they create their own concept books.

Materials:

- Copies of *City by Numbers* and *Alphabet City*, both by Stephen T. Johnson
- Drawing paper and pens or pencils
- Cameras (optional)

What to Do:

1. Show students the pictures from *City by Numbers* and *Alphabet City*, encouraging them to look carefully at the details of where the numbers and letters can be spotted.

2. Discuss the different ways the numbers and letters appear in buildings, in the landscape, and in common objects that we all recognize.

3. Send students out in pairs to search for numbers and letters found in the school. Tell them to draw what they see or take photos, if cameras are available.

4. Have students write a caption for each drawing or photo. Display their creations for the whole class to see. For example, if students see the number 8 created by two circular flower pots sitting side by side, the might write, "Look closely at the tops of these two pots and you'll see the number 8." Or maybe they spot the letter A on the side of a stepladder. This caption might say, "Look at the side of this stepladder. Do you see the letter A? We do!"

5. Organize the captioned drawings and photos in a logical sequence—numerically and alphabetically. Ask the students if there are other possible ways to organize them.

6. Display the drawings and photos in key locations around the school so other students and teachers learn to see details in the world around them.

Follow Up:

- Have older students help younger students find more examples of numbers and letters all around the school. The more you look, the more you see, and even the youngest eyes can be trained to find interesting details in the world around them.
- Take students on a field trip into town, the city, or out into the country to continue finding examples to add to their collections.

Focus Lesson Based On . . .

Click, Clack, Moo: Cows That Type

Doreen Cronin, Author
Betsy Lewin, Illustrator
Simon and Schuster, 2000
(See description on page 40.)

Target Trait: Organization
Secondary Traits: Word Choice, Voice

The cows in this text know how to get just what they want from poor Farmer Brown. In this humorous dialogue between animals and humans, much is exposed about all the characters. Students can use the repeating refrain, "Click, clack, moo," as an organizer as they write their own back-and-forth dialogue, applying the same skills that Cronin does.

Materials:

- A copy of *Click, Clack, Moo: Cows That Type*
- Overhead transparencies and markers
- Writing paper and pens or pencils

What to Do:

1. As a class, brainstorm a school rule that students would like to see changed, such as following the school dress code or being required to carry hall passes.

2. Have students work in one large group with you as the scribe at the overhead to write a proposal to the principal that includes:
   - A clear statement about what they want
   - Solid arguments for why the change should occur
   - What they would be willing to give up if their request is honored

3. Read *Click, Clack, Moo* to students. Discuss the different requests the cows and the ducks sent to the farmer. Point out how the book is organized: a request, a response—back and forth.

4. Put students into pairs and assign each of them a role as a student or the principal. Ask them to write a back-and-forth series of requests and responses from the point of view of their assigned role about the rule they would like to see changed at school. Remind them that each time the student request gets a response from the principal, they need to revise their next request. Then the principal needs to revise his or her response accordingly, too.

5. Have the students write back and forth three times, and then work with them to create a surprise ending that is similar to that in *Click, Clack, Moo*.

6. Encourage pairs of students to share their final requests and responses aloud with the group.

Follow Up:

- Submit the original class proposal to the principal and ask him or her to write back. Be sure to show the principal *Click, Clack, Moo* so that his or her response fits the organizational pattern. Once the students get the principal's response, allow them time to create a counterproposal and resubmit it.
- Invite the principal in to discuss the proposals and how effective they were in persuading him or her to reconsider the school rule.

FOCUS LESSON BASED ON . . .

Through My Eyes
Ruby Bridges, Author
Scholastic, 1999
(See description on page 39.)

Target Trait: Organization
Secondary Traits: Conventions, Ideas, Voice, Word Choice, Sentence Fluency, Presentation

This book, which centers on the childhood of civil rights activist Ruby Bridges, will inspire students to look at research in a whole new way. Made up of stories, essays, newspaper articles, poems, and other types of writing, this book is an excellent resource for use with a lesson that helps students see how to organize different forms of nonfiction writing that go beyond the traditional essay.

MATERIALS:

- A copy of *Through My Eyes*
- Overhead transparencies and markers
- Notebooks
- Print and electronic research sources
- Drawing paper and pens
- Writing paper and pens or pencils

WHAT TO DO:

1. Share *Through My Eyes* with the class. Make a list on the overhead projector of all the different types of writing in the book: quotations, stories, observations by third parties, captions, poems, and so on.

2. Discuss how using multiple types of writing to convey information can be interesting to readers.

3. Have students research an important person who is connected to something you're covering in a content area. Encourage them to use as many sources as possible.

4. Have students record their research in a notebook, devoting separate sections to different forms of writing. For example, if they discover a song lyric that works well, it goes in a section entitled "Music." Another section might be called "Personal Background and History." Important events that influenced the person's life can be placed in another section. Information on the historical context—a copy of a newspaper from that time, for example—could be placed in another section. As students find information about the person, they add it to their notebooks. Be sure to emphasize that gathering a variety of genres, as Ruby Bridges did to write *Through My Eyes*, is the goal. Keep the book handy so students can refer to it for ideas as they research.

5. Have a class meeting to sort all the information from the notebooks. Make a list of the different types of writing the students collected for each section, poetry, narration, newspaper articles, captions for pictures, essays, dialogue, advertisements, and so forth.

6. Hang all the pieces that students have written on a bulletin board organized around the sections of information they collected for the project.

FOLLOW UP:

- Encourage students to scan all the different pieces of information they collected into a computer file by section and create a collage of all of it on the computer. Add graphic elements.
- Share the results of the research with other students at the same grade level who might be studying the same subject.

Chapter Three

Sparking Voice

"Passion is to picture books as yeast is to bread: one is nothing without the other. . . . Writing without passion is writing for oblivion."

—Mem Fox
Dear Mem Fox, I Have Read All Your Books, Even the Pathetic Ones

Voice just jumps right out of good picture books—each one is so lively, engaging, and unique. If you ever doubted the power of voice in writing, spend a few minutes with some excellent picture books. Their energy will buoy the sagging spirit. The books in this chapter were chosen because they have lots of voice, but also because they represent a range of voices, from loud and boisterous to quiet and compassionate.

Voice: A Definition

Voice is the golden thread that runs through a piece of writing. It's how the reader knows it is really you speaking. Voice is the writer's music coming out through the words, the sense that a real person is speaking to you and cares about the message. It is the heart and soul of the writing, the magic, the wit, the feeling, the life and breath. It's flashes of spirit. When the writer is engaged personally with the topic, he or she imparts a personal flavor to the piece that is unmistakably his or hers alone. It is that individual something—different from the mark of all other writers—that we call "voice."

Try using this book and lesson to reinforce the trait of voice.

FEATURE FOCUS LESSON BASED ON . . .

Voices in the Park

Anthony Browne, Author and Illustrator

D.K. Publishing, 1998

(See description on page 62.)

Target Trait: Voice

Secondary Trait: Word Choice

Browne tells one story four times, from the perspective of a dominating woman, a depressed man, a lonely boy, and a sweet young girl who has a special way about her. What better way to illustrate how the voice in writing can change radically, depending on the point of view?

MATERIALS:

- A copy of *Voices in the Park*
- Chart paper or overhead transparencies and markers
- A short piece of writing with little or no voice made into a transparency. (See example below or examples in *6+1 Traits of Writing: The Complete Guide*, Scholastic, 2003.)
- Writing paper and pens or pencils

What to Do:

1. Read *Voices in the Park* to students.

2. Discuss each of the four narrators and list their personality traits on the chart or overhead.

3. Read aloud the short piece of writing on the transparency with little or no voice. You will use this piece as a springboard to add voice.

> **Example:**
>
> "Rip in the Pants" by a fifth grader
>
> Just about a week ago my teacher had a rip in his pants. It was really funny. I didn't see it right away but someone told me then I saw it and wanted to laugh but I held it in. Then someone told him and everyone started to laugh. Then he went home to change. The End.

4. Divide the class into small groups and identify possible points of view for the writing.

   Possible Points of View:

   - The student
   - The principal
   - The teacher
   - Another teacher
   - A student who liked the teacher
   - A student who didn't like the teacher
   - The pants

5. Assign a point of view to each group and ask members to brainstorm how the voice would change according to their assignment. For instance, what voice would be appropriate if a student wrote about his teacher's pants ripping compared to if the teacher himself wrote about it? Then ask groups to rewrite the story. Here are three examples by seventh-grade students:

From the Point of View of a Student in the Class:

Last week, my teacher Mr. Carroll had a colossal tear in the back of his pants. It happened when his pants got caught on the chalkboard edge. At first, I didn't notice it, but then my friend told me. We wanted to laugh at his bright pink boxers. We giggled, and he asked us what was so funny. We told him, and his face turned brighter than his boxers. He ran to the office to get Mrs. Holladay to sub for a while as he ran home to get changed. The whole class burst into laughter and people had tears falling down their cheeks. We talked about it the rest of class. The next day he was very quiet and stayed as far away as possible from the chalkboard. He told us not to tell anyone. He would be the laughingstock of the school, the punch line in the teachers' lounge! Too late.

From the Point of View of the Teacher:

Rip. I didn't think much of it. Kids are always ripping something.
I continued to teach. Giggle, snicker, snicker. I didn't think much of it. Students get off task. I addressed it, and continued to teach. I felt a draft. I didn't think much of it, until I realized there shouldn't be a draft, especially there. I continued to teach. A slow tingling, horrifying realization. The rip was from me and my pants—in a place it shouldn't be. The laughs were *at* me and my new drafty trousers. The red burned slowly from my neck to my forehead. My eyes met theirs. "Well," I said, "just get over it."

From the Point of View of the Pants:

This is not right. I wasn't made to be worn by a guy this big. Oww! Every time he does anything but stand still, I hurt. I'm pinched and mushed and cramped so tight I can hardly breathe. I need relief. What I really want is revenge. I know . . . rrrrrip! Ha! That'll show him. But wait, what happens next? Maybe he'll just throw me out and I'll never see the light of day again. Man, oh man, if I'd only been a tie, then I could've just choked him!

Follow Up:

- Read a different story and think of how it might change depending on who is telling it and for what purpose.
- Explore all the possible voices for new pieces of writing. Using samples of student writing that need work, invite students to add the details that will reveal the voice.

Picture Books for Sparking Voice

The Babe & I

David A. Adler, Author
Terry Widener, Illustrator
Harcourt, 1999

Told from the point of view of a young boy during the Great Depression, the story deals with the hard reality of a son watching his father lose his job and how he helps his family through the toughest of times. He and his best friend Jacob decide to sell newspapers, but not on just any street corner. They sell them on the walking route to Yankee Stadium, and their business thrives. One day the great Babe Ruth himself buys a newspaper from the boy and tells him to keep the change from a five-dollar bill, which allows the two of them to go to the game. From that point on, the young boy realizes that he and Babe are a team, just like he and his father are. Both are working together through hard times. This is a poignant piece about a time in our history when "down and out" took on a new meaning.

Wolf!

Becky Bloom, Author
Pascal Biet, Illustrator
Orchard Books, 1999

Once you take a look at this book, you will want to share it with all your friends. What could be more enjoyable than the story of the big, bad wolf told through the eyes of educated barnyard animals? Educated? Yes, in this story they read. It's a delightful romp, intended to put the wolf in his place through the power of literacy. This would be a great piece to use in combination with more traditional versions of *The Three Little Pigs*. The voice is energetic and fun—a delicious and delectable reading treat. See focus lesson on page 78.

Voices in the Park

Anthony Browne, Author and Illustrator
DK Publishing, 1998

This complex book is about how four different people perceive their day at the park. As the story shifts from character to character, the reader gets an inside look at how an event can be interpreted quite differently depending on the storyteller's point of view. Browne's illustrations are quite unusual, too. Detailed and highly stylized, the reader is drawn into this piece quite naturally. See focus lesson on page 59.

Gleam and Glow

Eve Bunting, Author

Peter Sylvada, Illustrator

Harcourt, 2001

I'm such a fan of Eve Bunting. I have never seen a book of hers that didn't tackle tough issues with great insight, respect for the reader, and great care for the topic. This time, she takes on the hardships of war. As a mother and her children hurry to leave their home before the invasion of hostile forces, the young boy who is telling the story reaches for his two little fish, Gleam and Glow. Of course they cannot come, and in one poignant scene, the boy leaves them with a bit of food. "I sprinkled what was left of their food on the water. 'One or two extra days of life,' I whispered." This piece has a nice wrap-up, too, but the reader will be enthralled all the way.

The Frog Principal

Stephanie Calmenson, Author

Denise Brunkus, Illustrator

Scholastic, 2001

Remember the story of the Frog Prince told by the Brothers Grimm? This time it's the assistant principal who is the frog, and, oh, what a hard time the children have with him. Their principal "goes away" and in his place comes a slimy, green frog. What happens next is funny and original, and the voice is delightful. It's a nice example of how an author can write a funny piece without overwriting it. This twist on a familiar story should inspire young writers to come up with their own versions.

Little Yau: A Fuzzhead Tale

Janell Cannon, Author and Illustrator

Harcourt, 2002

Heartfelt, sweet, compassionate. With this book, Cannon scores big in voice. How can a reader resist Little Yau and the other Fuzzheads when most of the book is the search for an herb to cure one of their own who lies dying? And, when the search takes them into the land of people, you have to hold your breath and hope that it will all turn out well. Several intermingled themes work well here—friendship, growing up, and child/adult relationships.

We the Kids: The Preamble to the Constitution of the United States

David Catrow, Author and Illustrator

Dial Books, 2002

The text here is literally the preamble to the Constitution, which probably makes the book sound terribly dry. But what makes it special is how the author sets up the text. He begins with a witty, kid-friendly preface to let readers know that he, too, once thought the Preamble was archaic—like so many historical documents, written by a bunch of stuffy old guys many, many years ago. That was, until he started reading. Really reading—and understanding the Preamble's powerful message. He also includes a lively, equally kid-friendly glossary right up front to ease the reading. And the illustrations are dynamite—lively and alive with color and action. See focus lesson on page 75.

Blood & Gore

Vicki Cobb, Author and Illustrator

Scholastic, 1997

"Blood and gore are hidden as long as your skin is not broken. Your amazing skin keeps your insides inside you and the dangers of the outside from getting in." So begins the section on skin in this informative and fascinating book. The book is written in an authoritative voice, and readers will find themselves turning from one interesting fact-filled page about the body to the next. With brilliant color illustrations and text in just the right-sized bites, this book is bound to be a favorite with readers who are intrigued by how their insides work. This book works great for the traits of word choice too.

The Prince of Butterflies

Bruce Coville, Author

John Clapp, Illustrator

Harcourt, 2002

A lovely combination of reality and fantasy, this book about the special bond between a boy and monarch butterflies will teach as well as entertain. The conversation between the boy and the butterflies about the lack of green space due to the development of malls and parking lots is powerful and moving. This book is a celebration of life and a treatise on how important it is to follow your dreams.

Diary of a Worm

Doreen Cronin, Author

Harry Bliss, Illustrator

Joanna Cotler Books, 2003

The insights about life told through this little earthworm's writing is guaranteed to tickle you and your students. In one of my favorite passages, the worm tells his vain older sister that she's wasting her time gazing at herself in the mirror because her face looks just like her rear end. In another, when he decides to use good manners, he winds up saying "good morning" to six hundred ants. Whew! That's a lot. From the first page to the last, Cronin captures this charming little earthworm's voice as she parallels the everyday lives of humans and insects.

The Spider and the Fly

Tony DiTerlizzi, Author and Illustrator

Simon and Schuster, 2002

This 2002 Caldecott winner is certainly deserving of the award. It's not a book to share with students who are afraid of spiders, however. Because it is so brilliantly illustrated, it would only reinforce those fears. My favorite part is at the end, where the spider writes to the reader. It begins, "No doubt you've finished our delicious tale and are surprised by this little tragedy, but then again, what did you expect from a story about a spider and a fly? Happily ever after?" The letter, coupled with the classic poem of the same name written in the early 1800s, is a study in contrasting voices—each powerful in its own way. See focus lesson on page 82.

Rachel: The Story of Rachel Carson

Amy Ehrlich, Author

Wendell Minor, Illustrator

Harcourt, 2003

Rachel Carson's brilliant book, *Silent Spring*, is, in my eyes, the most significant plea ever written for environmental education and understanding. First published in 1962, it is filled with passion and beautiful language, which places it a cut above other books on environmental issues. With this book, children can learn about Rachel Carson and her powerful and important work. Ehrlich paints a tribute to this pioneer of environmental writing, and helps us appreciate her contributions in whole new ways.

Testing Miss Malarkey

Judy Finchler, Author

Kevin O'Malley, Illustrator

Walker and Company, 2000

There isn't a teacher or administrator in schools today who won't get a chuckle out of this book. The standardized testing phenomenon is a part of our everyday lives. This book focuses on the pressure on all of us for students to score high, while providing a generous dose of wit and satire. It is clever and contemporary, and certainly finds a soft spot in our hearts and minds. I especially love the acronym for test, I.P.T.U. Now, is Finchler referring to the students or the adults?

How Are You Peeling? Foods with Moods

Saxton Freymann, Author and Illustrator

Scholastic, 1999

Foods with Moods. Isn't that a great subtitle? Using brightly colored, large photographs, Freymann presents, on each page spread, two contrasting moods for each piece of fruit or vegetable. For example, the orange is sneaky and cowed. The cantaloupe is shown as the shell of a turtle-like creature and asks the question, "How are you when friends drop by? [photo with head sticking out] / With someone new . . . a little shy? [photo with head tucked in]" Each pair poses a new combination of voices, moods, feelings, and emotions. It's the perfect book to help students get beyond stale words and bring freshness and originality to their own writing. A clever piece that will appeal to all ages. Perfect to use for Presentation, too.

Harvesting Hope: The Story of Cesar Chavez

Kathleen Krull, Author

Yuyi Morales, Illustrator

Harcourt, 2003

This book strikes a thoughtful chord with the reader. The author goes beyond a simple restating of what happened in Cesar Chavez's life and gets into Chavez's deeply held belief that things could change for migrant farm workers, and he could be the agent of that change. The passion of this great man is felt on every page. His transformation from a shy, soft-spoken child to a man who could move groups to action by his carefully chosen words is a subject worthy of study.

There's a Hair in My Dirt!

Gary Larson, Author and Illustrator

HarperPerennial, 1998

Gary, Gary, Gary. This is one of the most enjoyed books in my collection. Every time I take it to a workshop and I hear a burst of laughter from across the room, I know it's because a group of teachers is reading it. The premise is simple and wonderful: Suppose you are a worm. What bugs you? What can you tell us about your poor, pathetic life? Larson uses his black and sardonic humor to teach and entertain us at the same time. What you learn about invertebrates sneaks up on you as you delight in the plot, the characters, the dilemmas, and the richness of voice.

Alaska's Three Pigs

Arlene Laverde, Author

Mindy Dwyer, Illustrator

Sasquatch Books, 2000

This is the classic story of the Three Little Pigs set in, of all places, Alaska. Instead of the Big, Bad Wolf, they have to deal with a hungry grizzly bear! These pigs love the outdoors and have wonderful adventures skiing, snowboarding, and dog sledding. But the fun ends when they realize that they have to build their houses before winter strikes. See how each pig uses indigenous materials to build his house and how, as a team, they outsmart the hungry bear. This would be a great book as part of a larger study on Alaska and how we adapt to cold climates. You can use this book to compliment the lesson at the end of this chapter based on *Wolf!*

Why Heaven Is Far Away

Julius Lester, Author

Joe Cepeda, Illustrator

Scholastic, 2002

This book is a riot. Treating some of life's more serious issues in a lighthearted and entertaining way, Lester explains why Earth and Heaven are so far away—and in this book, snakes get all the blame. And, he explains the first commandment (which is actually the Zero Commandment with ten others to come): "Thou Shalt Talk and Listen to Thy Neighbor." The world would be a better place if Julius Lester had his way. The playfulness of this piece is an easy way to open the door to discuss serious subjects.

Walking with Henry: Based on the Life and Works of Henry David Thoreau

Thomas Locker, Author and Illustrator

Fulcrum Publisher, 2002

In this book, the voice is strongest in the illustrations—not the text. Although Henry David Thoreau's life and important beliefs are summarized beautifully, it is the text coupled with extraordinary pictures that bring the author's voice to life. Thoreau's belief that "In Wilderness is the preservation of the world . . ." is exquisitely captured in Locker's art. This is a picture book that is worth the price for the pictures alone.

The Lady in the Box

Ann McGovern, Author

Marni Backer, Illustrator

Turtle Books, 1997

Homelessness. Many books have been written to address this topic—and this is an excellent example. Two young children come to know a destitute woman who lives in a cardboard box near their home. At first, they are scared of her, but eventually they realize that they must do something to help. Compassionate and caring, this piece pairs well with another favorite on the topic, *Fly Away Home* by Eve Bunting. The authors' two voices are similar and yet unique, and the stories have completely different outcomes.

How Whales Walked Into the Sea

Faith McNulty, Author

Ted Rand, Illustrator

Scholastic, 1999

How did whales come into being? How did they migrate from earth to sea? Drawing upon our fascination with these magnificent creatures, the author develops a theory of how the whales came to be sea mammals. This book would be a fantastic compliment to a more traditional text on the topic. Although the facts may be the same, younger and older readers alike will be more able to understand the origin of whales in Faith McNulty's version because it is so full of voice.

Edward and the Pirates

David McPhail, Author and Illustrator

Little, Brown, 1997

Never forgot the power of books to let our imaginations soar. That is the message of *Edward and the Pirates*. Edward discovers that reading can take him anywhere—from racing dog sleds with Admiral Peary to running from the Sheriff of Nottingham in the

Sherwood Forest. One night in Edward's dreams, pirates come to life and tell him to hand over the book he is reading; they think it will tell them where their buried treasure lies. But, sadly, because the pirates don't know how to read, the book won't help them much. As Edward helps them, they discover together that the real treasure is knowing how to read.

I Wish Tonight

Lois Rock, Author

Anne Wilson, Illustrator

Good Books, 1999

"I wish." We all say those two simple little words so often. The wishes in this book are for things that make our world happier, safer, and better for all people. Students will appreciate examples of how we can learn to live together in peace—and perhaps be inspired to write some additional wishes of their own using the power of their voices to catch the reader up in their new ideas.

Grody's Not So Golden Rules

Nicole Rubel, Author and Illustrator

Harcourt, 2003

Tongue in cheek from beginning to end, this book is a delightful twist on the rules that many children live by every day. Little Grody turns motherly "suggestions," such as "You'd better straighten up your room," into more acceptable ones: "Don't bother putting your clothes away. They will be easier to find if you leave them out!" All children will enjoy Grody's version of the rules, and will want to add a few of their own!

The Bird House

Cynthia Rylant, Author

Barry Moser, Illustrator

Scholastic, 1998

A feeling, a tone, a special sense envelops you from the first page of this magical text. A young girl living alone, depressed and scared, is drawn into the light by the beauty of the birds living around her. As she watches them, they lift her spirits—except for the great barn owl who just sits and watches her. However, one day, that changes and, in turn, transforms the young girl's life forever. As you read this book, let its voice take you away to a natural world where birds can heal and help a girl discover a whole new life.

The Relatives Came

Cynthia Rylant, Author
Stephen Gammell, Illustrator
Aladdin Paperbacks, 1985

Summer vacation carries with it a feel and texture all its own. This book captures that mood, tone, and voice of these carefree days. When relatives come to visit we experience the joy of family vacations, somehow forgetting things like age-old squabbles, the insufferable cousin, and the smelly dog. We appreciate what's really important about families as the author relates this story about a time when relatives, young and old, unite in hugs and laughter.

A Symphony of Whales

Steve Schuch, Author
Peter Sylvada, Illustrator
Harcourt, 1999

This dramatic rescue story of a group of whales trapped in a frozen inlet reminds us all of our connection to nature. In this book we discover that music plays a part in creating the voice of the whales as they communicate and support each other. Based on a true story, *A Symphony of Whales* is a miracle of life. See focus lesson on page 76.

My Secret Camera: Life in the Lodz Ghetto

Frank Dabba Smith, Author
Mendel Grossman, Illustrator
Harcourt, 2000

Bravery, hardship, and the struggle for life are chronicled in this collection of black-and-white photographs taken during the Nazi occupation of Liz Shetto, Poland. The extended photo captions tell the story of the citizens of this city and how Mendel Grossman risked his life to capture the whole occupation in photos. The reader feels the pain of the townspeople. This simple but powerful book makes a lasting impression.

Just the Two of Us

Will Smith, Author
Kadir Nelson, Illustrator
Scholastic, 2001

I picked up this book innocently one day, not even noticing the author's name—Will Smith (yes, *the* Will Smith). I read the foreword and felt tears well up inside me. I read on. The passion, love, and deep commitment of this father to his son are overwhelming. A two, if not three, handkerchief book.

Beverly Billingsly Takes a Bow

Alexander Stadler, Author and Illustrator

Harcourt, 2003

Imagine the horror that Beverly feels when, while trying out for the school play, she opens her mouth and nothing comes out. Given a smaller part with only one line, Beverly is more than ready to give it her best on opening night. However, her most shining moment comes when she bravely steps in for a classmate who comes down with a bad case of stage fright. Her empathy for her friend and a thoughtful gift just when it is needed make Beverly Billingsly a very lovable character. In this simple story, Stadler uses a sweet and compassionate voice to show us the meaning of true friendship.

The Snow Bear

Liliana Stafford, Author

Lambert Davis, Illustrator

Scholastic, 2001

This story of a boy and a polar bear is simply told. The reality of their life in the Inuit village—how villagers must hunt bears to survive—is not sugar-coated. The voice is authentic because the author truly knows the ways of the Inuit natives. I was struck by how beautiful a person this protagonist is—real and kind. Brunn befriends a starving bear, and they learn to live together in the wild. Years later, Brunn runs into the bear again. Starving and old, Brunn is faced with the choice of killing the bear or helping him survive one last winter. When I turned the final page, I took a deep breath.

My Big Dog

Janet Stevens and Susan Stevens Crummel, Authors

Janet Stevens, Illustrator

A Golden Book, 1999

Point of view is a key consideration in voice. And from the title, you probably assume that this story is told from the point of view of the owner of a big dog. But in reality, it's told from a cat's point of view—a cat named Meryl whose perfect life is disrupted by a wiggly, noisy, slurpy, and clumsy puppy. Imagine the disdain of the cat who had everything—dish, sofa, chair, toy mouse, and bed—adjusting to this unwelcome addition to the family. After trying everything to get rid of the dog, Meryl has no choice but to leave. What follows is a series of events that eventually brings the cat back asking the question, "Could we be friends?"

The Little Red Hen (Makes a Pizza)

Philemon Sturges, Author

Amy Walrod, Illustrator

Dutton Children's Books, 1999

Lively, funny, and clever, this little red hen makes a pizza with about as much help as the original little red hen who made the bread. Contemporary but true to the classic story, students and adults will delight in the timeless message of working in cooperation to meet shared goals. The ending brings a charming surprise. You might want to compare and contrast voice in the two versions of the story.

Hooray for Diffendoofer Day!

Dr. Seuss and Jack Prelutsky, Authors

Lane Smith, Illustrator

Alfred A. Knopf, 1998

How do you encourage and support the teacher who is "different-er" than the rest—the one whose true voice shines through every day? You know the one? She or he is always a bit off—but her students are the ones who are learning the most. This book was begun by Dr. Seuss before his death and completed by Jack Prelutsky and Lane Smith. It catches the texture and flavor of teachers who really have it together. In Diffendoofer School, teachers are encouraged to be original and not worry about "the test" because they've taught the students how to learn. Teachers everywhere who dare to be different, who listen to their own voices in teaching and care more about uncovering than covering, should rejoice in this tribute.

Lest We Forget: The Passage from Africa to Slavery and Emancipation

Velma Maia Thomas, Author

Crown Publishers, 1997

Rich with original source materials from the Black Holocaust Museum in Milwaukee, Wisconsin, this three-dimensional text is one that can't be missed. This piece walks students through a dark time in history, when people were treated like animals, taken from their homeland and forced to work as slaves in colonial United States. Letters that open, pages that turn out, a copy of a slave receipt, newspaper ads for slave auctions, and even a fold-out cutaway drawing of a slave ship are included, along with detailed significant information about this historical time. When readers hold this text, they are reverent. They touch and read the pages silently. As they put the book down, they often touch it one more time as if to say, "We must remember." This is the kind of text that models voice in nonfiction that is passionate, powerful, and credible.

Mary Geddy's Day: A Colonial Girl in Williamsburg

Kate Waters, Author

Russ Kendall, Photographer

Scholastic, 1999

Told from the point of view of young Mary Geddy, this story is about a time in history that changed the future of America. We rarely read history written in the first person, and we even more rarely read it through female eyes, so this piece is a treasure. The energy and excitement Mary feels as she waits for election results that will determine whether the Virginia colony gains independence from Great Britain is infectious. The pros and cons of this decision, and how they are weighed by this child, make this an important addition to a U.S. history study.

Touchdown Mars!

Peggy Wethered and Ken Edgett, Authors

Michael Chesworth, Illustrator

G.P. Putnam's Sons, 2000

Written in two voices, one expressive and one more academic, this book is good to use to help students see how important it is to have a clear sense of purpose and audience when they write. Each page has two effective styles blending narrative and expository texts to create a voice that is both factually credible and fascinating to read. This would be an interesting format for students to try in their own writing.

Let the Celebrations BEGIN!

Margaret Wild, Author

Julie Vivas, Illustrator

Orchard Paperbacks, 1991

The optimistic voice of children is what may strike you most as you read this book. Though they are harbored in a Nazi concentration camp where survival is an everyday struggle, the children make toys out of the bits of life they find around them—old yarn, rags, thread, remembrances of their old lives. They understand, with an intuition that only children have, that liberation is near and a return to life is just around the corner. The children tell about and celebrate their dreams of a new life as they spend their last days in the camp. This is a poignant text that speaks honestly from the first word to the last.

Dumpy La Rue

Elizabeth Winthrop, Author

Betsy Lewin, Illustrator

Henry Holt and Company, 2001

What do you do with a pig that wants to dance? You let him, of course! That's the happy ending for Dumpy La Rue. But he doesn't get to dance until he convinces his parents and all the other barnyard animals that wanting to dance isn't strange. It is fun. A pig ought to be able to do what he wants and what he's good at, right? This darling story is affirming for children. It helps them to realize that if they take a risk and try something different, it's more than okay. This is the same understanding that writers need to embrace to have voice in their writing. It's the only way to go for them and for Dumpy La Rue, the pig who knew what he wanted to do. See focus lesson on page 80.

Sweet Dream Pie

Audrey Wood, Author

Mark Teague, Illustrator

Scholastic Inc., 1998

"By noon, the delicious smell of Ma Brindle's Sweet Dream Pie blanketed the neighborhood with a blissful aroma." This enchanting story weaves a web of sweetness around readers and draws them in with delicious descriptions of a pie made of chocolate, gumdrops, and every sugary ingredient you can imagine. The rich, descriptive text bubbles and oozes right along with Ma Brindle's pie as readers are folded into a world of dreams and indulgences. Gentle, kind, and loving, the text is written in a voice that is warm and welcoming.

The Other Side

Jacqueline Woodson, Author

Earl B. Lewis, Illustrator

G.P. Putnam's Sons, 2001

The simple eloquence of this book will take your breath away. Woodson uses a fence as a metaphor for racism in a story about two young girls, one white and one black, who live on opposites sides of that fence, yet come to know each other despite it. Their mothers have warned them not to go over the fence, but that doesn't mean they can't sit on the fence. And so their summer is spent talking about all the things that friends share. The voice of the book is slow and graceful like summer. There is something so perfect about it—it is real, important, and inspiring. "Someday somebody's going to come along and knock this old fence down." We most certainly are ready for that day to arrive.

Focus Lessons for Sparking Voice

Focus Lesson Based On . . .

We the Kids: The Preamble to the Constitution of the United States

David Catrow, Author and Illustrator

Dial Books, 2002

(See description on page 64.)

Target Trait: Voice

Secondary Traits: Word Choice, Ideas, Sentence Fluency

Materials:

- A copy of *We the Kids: The Preamble to the Constitution of the United States*
- Thesauruses
- Overhead transparencies and markers
- Large sheet of butcher paper
- Writing paper and pens or pencils

With this lesson, students study the language of the Preamble to the Constitution, which may seem a bit archaic to them. They read the document for its voice and then for its powerful and timeless ideas. Thanks to this author, terms such as *posterity* and *domestic tranquility* are explained so even young readers will understand their meaning. The lively illustrations underscore the meaning of the text and provide some much appreciated voice and sparkle. This lesson is a mini-study on old-world and new-world voices.

What to Do:

1. On an overhead transparency, list the words in the glossary at the front of Catrow's book.

2. Ask students to define the ones they know and make good guesses on the others.

3. Ask students how many words and phrases from the Preamble are not used today. Discuss changes in language from the 1700s to today.

4. Give a copy of a thesaurus to small groups of students and assign them a set of words to look up that come from the Preamble. Make a list of synonyms for the more archaic words. Then, have groups combine their lists to create one big one that can be hung at the front of the room.

5. Read aloud *We the Kids: The Preamble to the Constitution of the United States*. Discuss the important ideas in the Preamble based on the author's Preamble foreword and students' own interpretations.

6. As a class, rewrite the Preamble using contemporary words and phrases to replace the more archaic ones. Compare the two versions.

7. Discuss the voice in both versions and come up with words to describe each one. For the traditional version, you might come up with *stodgy*, *serious*, and *formal*. For the new version, you might say *thoughtful*, *powerful*, and *serious*. Do students like the sound of the version with more formal words or more familiar words? How does the choice of the words affect the voice?

Follow Up:

- Get copies of other important documents, such as the Declaration of Independence or the Gettysburg Address, and examine them for words that need explaining in today's world.
- Ask students to "translate" these documents into more contemporary language so younger readers can understand them.

Focus Lesson Based On . . .

A Symphony of Whales
Steve Schuch, Author
Peter Sylvada, Illustrator
Harcourt, 1999
(See description on page 70.)

Target Trait: Voice
Secondary Traits: Word Choice, Ideas, Organization

Did you know that beluga whales are naturally drawn to classical music? In fact, marine scientists have found that such music helps in leading them to the open sea when they are trapped and, as such, can save their lives. Focusing on favorite types of music can help students, too—it can help them understand the trait of voice. In this lesson, students write a story with a plan for saving a favorite animal, using music as one of components of their plan.

MATERIALS:

- A copy of *A Symphony of Whales*
- Writing paper and pens or pencils
- Internet access for research

WHAT TO DO:

1. Have students list three types of music they like best, such as hip-hop, country, and rock.

2. Have students write a paragraph describing each type of music and what they like about it, including favorite singers and songs. Encourage students to use the Internet to research exact titles and names.

3. Read *A Symphony of Whales* aloud.

4. As a class, discuss why, according to Schuch, classical music is the whale's favorite music.

5. Have students put themselves in Glashka's shoes and envision a different type of animal becoming trapped. Using *A Symphony of Whales* as their model, have them create a story with a plan to rescue the animals that includes their favorite kind of music. What kind of animal are they saving? How did it get trapped? What specific songs did they play to try to get it free?

6. Share the stories and discuss the different voices in each.

FOLLOW UP:

- Ask students to imagine that other whales like music as the belugas do in this story. Discuss the many types of whales there are in the world. Do students think they all like classical music? How about orcas or humpbacks? Ask students to select the kind of music they think each whale would like and write a paragraph explaining their choice.

- Now think about other marine animals such as sea lions, dolphins, or sharks. Do students think they respond to music like whales do? Discuss. Then allow time for students to research and write about their findings.

FOCUS LESSON BASED ON . . .

Wolf!

Becky Bloom, Author
Pascal Biet, Illustrator
Orchard Books, 1999
(See description on page 62.)

Target Trait: Voice
Secondary Traits: Ideas, Word Choice

Voice jumps out when the point of view from which the story is being told changes. Since most students are familiar with famous fairy tales, they are an excellent model for working on voice. This book, a take-off on *The Three Little Pigs*, is one example of many picture books in which the author takes an old story and gives it some interesting twists and turns to create a new one.

MATERIALS:

- A copy of *Wolf!*
- *The Three Little Pigs* and other fairy tales
- *The True Story of the Three Little Pigs* by Jon Scieszka
- Overhead transparencies and markers
- Writing paper and pens or pencils

WHAT TO DO:

1. Discuss the genre of fairy tales with students. Ask them to name their favorites and talk about the familiar story elements in each one, such as the wolf and the lost little girl in *The Three Little Pigs*.

2. Read the traditional version of *Three Little Pigs* and discuss the voices that students notice. Are they warm and friendly? Distant and frightening? Academic? Humorous? See if students can identify the most prominent voice.

3. Read *Wolf!* aloud. Discuss the story elements that changed between the two versions and those that stayed the same. Were many of the characters the same in both stories? Were the plot points similar or the same? Was the setting the same? And was the ending of the story the same or different?

4. Ask students to identify the voice in *Wolf!* Is it the same or different than the one in the traditional version? What is the difference between the two?

5. Create a chart on the overhead that compares the voice in the traditional version with the voice in the new story.

Voices from *Wolf!*	Voices from *The Three Little Pigs*
Patronizing	Honest
Aloof	Scared
Confident	Nervous
Positive	Determined

6. Read *The True Story of the Three Little Pigs* by Jon Scieszka and contrast its voice with the traditional version of *The Three Little Pigs*. List responses as you did for the first two books.

7. Ask students to select a traditional fairy tale and write a new version, just as Bloom and Scieszka did. Ideally, students should work in small groups because the discussion will promote ideas for their story and the voice(s) in which they write it.

FOLLOW UP:

- Have students illustrate their stories and share them with younger students at school.
- Turn the stories into scripts and have students perform their "fractured fairy tale" plays. Be sure to allow plenty of rehearsal time beforehand.

Focus Lesson Based On . . .

Dumpy La Rue

Elizabeth Winthrop, Author

Betsy Lewin, Illustrator

Henry Holt and Company, 2001

(See description on page 74.)

Target Trait: Voice

Secondary Traits: Word Choice, Organization

Imagine a pig who wants to dance! That's Dumpy La Rue, "the pig who knew what he wanted to do." No matter how much his family refused to believe that Dumpy could learn to dance, he knew he had it in him. In this lesson, students concentrate on finding their own voices in writing, just as Dumpy La Rue found his passion in dance.

Materials:

- A copy of *Dumpy La Rue*
- Overhead transparencies and markers; chart paper and markers; or chalkboard and chalk
- Writing paper and pens or pencils

What to Do:

1. Ask students to make a list of five things they would like to learn how to do, but think will be very hard.

2. Have them choose the most challenging item from the list.

3. Ask students to write three or four reasons why learning this activity will be difficult. For example, if a student writes, "I want to learn how to do a back flip in gymnastics," her reasons for why it is difficult may include:
    - It will take a lot of practice.
    - I will need a lot of physical strength.
    - I will need to be more flexible than I am now.
    - I will need to overcome my fear of doing a back flip.

4. Have students create a list of three or four motivating comments to read when they need encouragement. For example:
   - I can do this; I can do anything if I keep trying.
   - It's important to follow through with your goals.
   - I will feel so good the first time I do a perfect back flip. Everyone will be so proud of me.

5. Read *Dumpy La Rue* to the class.

6. Create a short list of encouraging statements for Dumpy La Rue to follow as he learns how to dance. Compare these statements to the negative ones that other characters in the book make. Discuss the value of having positive support when attempting difficult things.

7. Discuss how Dumpy took on a hard task even though his family didn't believe in him. Ask: "Do you think Dumpy took a risk when he taught himself how to dance? What kind of risk? Was he afraid of what others might think?"

8. Ask students if the risk Dumpy took is like the risk writers take when they write with voice. Encourage students to look at a piece of their own writing and see if it has voice. Ask: "Have you taken any risks with your writing by choosing new words, coming up with fresh and original details, or trying a new way to organize?" Remind them that writing with voice is how you let readers know how you think and feel—like Dumpy La Rue did when he danced.

Follow Up:

- Create a list of motivating bulletin board comments on voice that students can turn to when they need them, such as *This sounds just like you!*; *What an unusual way to look at this*; *It made me think*; *I feel like I know this person*; *This piece begs to be read aloud*; *Your piece is not like anyone else's*; *I appreciate that*; *Your confidence as a writer makes a big difference to me as a reader*; *I can identify with this point of view.*

- Ask students to write in their writer's notebooks about times when they've shown perseverance like Dumpy La Rue, and reflect on what they learned from that experience.

Focus Lesson Based On . . .

The Spider and the Fly

Tony DiTerlizzi, Author and Illustrator
Simon and Schuster, 2002
(See description on page 65.)

Target Trait: Voice
Secondary Traits: Organization, Word Choice

This Caldecott Award–winning version of the traditional poem is a visual wonder. As I was reading it, however, I was struck by the difference in voice between the main body of the book and the letter from the spider at the end of the book: the former being dark and tense, and the latter being sarcastic and humorous. The purpose of this lesson is to study these contrasting voices. Students will understand more about the trait of voice as they describe the two voices in this book.

Materials:

- Copies of *The Spider and the Fly* for use in groups of three to four students
- Overhead transparencies and markers
- Writing paper and pens or pencils

What to Do:

1. Ask students what stories or poems they have read that stick in their minds because the voice was so powerful. From there, ask them to rank the importance of voice in writing on a scale of 1 to 5 (1 being lowest, 5 being highest).

2. Read *The Spider and the Fly* to students, without showing them the pictures. Ask them how much voice it has and see if they can find adjectives to describe the voice.

3. Put students in small groups and give each group a copy of the book. Ask students to pay close attention to the pictures to determine if they add to their understanding of the idea and the voice.

4. Discuss the role of pictures in understanding an idea and creating a voice.

5. Ask groups to read the letter from the spider at the end of the book and see if they can describe the voice, using adjectives.

6. As a whole class, summarize by creating three columns for voices in this work: one for the text by itself, one for the illustrations, and one for the letter at the end.

The Spider and the Fly by Tony DiTerlizzi		
Voice in the text	**Voice in the illustrations**	**Voice in the endpapers**
Formal Scary Persuasive	Mesmerizing Captivating Illustrative	Sarcastic Wicked Ego-centered

7. Now ask students to revisit their original 1-to-5 scores on the importance of voice in writing. Do they retain their scores or change them based on what they have learned?

Follow Up:

- Ask students to read different sections of a newspaper such as the front page, the obituaries, and the editorial page, and rate the voice of each. Students may find that some sections such as the editorials, cartoons, and columns have more voice than others. Discuss.
- Create a wall chart of descriptors for voice such as *bold, hilarious, contemplative,* and *judgmental*, and have students refer to them as they write. Add descriptors as you discover them in examples of writing.

Chapter Four

Expanding Word Choice

"Boy! Why can't we have Boy tonight? We never have Boy anymore! . . . Boy Chops, a big Baked Boy-tato, and some Boys-n-Berry Pie."

—Bob Hartman
The Wolf Who Cried Boy

The language of picture books can be stunningly beautiful, delightful, hilarious, momentous, and flat-out grand, which is quite an accomplishment, considering that authors of picture books do not have that many words to work with. Each one must be carefully selected for its clarity and ability to create images, sounds, textures, and feelings. Working with words and working with pictures is a natural, powerful combination.

Word Choice: A Definition

"The conclusion is simple. Picture books can do just about everything other kinds of books can do, and in the vibrations between words and pictures, sometimes more."

—Barbara Bader
The Horn Book Magazine

Word choice is more than just about the use—or misuse—of words. It is also about the use of rich, colorful, precise language that communicates not just in a functional way, but also in a way that moves and enlightens the reader. In good descriptive writing, strong word choice clarifies and expands ideas. In persuasive writing, it moves you to a new vision of things. In narrative writing, it creates images in your mind that are so real, you feel like you are part of the story itself. Once students have learned the basics about word choice, steer them toward using exceptional, beautiful language and toward using everyday words well.

Here is a lesson based on a book by one of my favorite authors to get you thinking about the trait of word choice.

FEATURE FOCUS LESSON BASED ON . . .

Hello, Harvest Moon
Ralph Fletcher, Author
Kate Kiesler, Illustrator
Houghton Mifflin, 2003
(See description on page 87.)

Target Trait: Word Choice
Secondary Traits: Voice, Ideas

MATERIALS:

- A copy of *Hello, Harvest Moon*
- Overhead transparencies and markers
- Writing paper and pens or pencils

This quiet book features lush, lyrical paintings and language to match. The structure of the lesson is to look at the craft by pulling out exemplary passages from *Hello, Harvest Moon*. Students will learn to stay with a topic longer by stretching the language—saying something in a way that calls upon many senses. They will display these passages and try to write pieces like it, using Fletcher's work as a model.

WHAT TO DO:

1. Ask students what they know about the moon and its cycles, and then have them tell you all the phrases containing the word *moon* that they know: "moonstruck," "once in a blue moon," "moon over Miami," "moonbeam," and so on. If "harvest moon" isn't on their list, add it.

2. Ask students to research these phrases in small groups and report their findings to the whole class. Make sure that "harvest moon" is part of the research.

3. Read *Hello, Harvest Moon* aloud. Discuss the book's ideas and then ask students if they think Fletcher's word choice is strong.

4. Read the book again. Ask students to write down phrases that they particularly enjoy. They may choose phrases such as "Hello, harvest moon," "silent slippers," "staining earth and sky with a ghostly glow," "double-dipped in moonlight," "like tiny moonlings floating up to their mother," and "cloaked in moonshadow."

5. Have students read the phrases to each other and select their top five favorites.

6. Analyze each favorite to determine what the author did to create a vivid image. Was it a simile or metaphor? Alliteration? Personification? A particularly specific noun? One or two favorites might contain an action verb. Whatever the technique, help students to see that creative word choice makes the writing interesting and powerful.

7. Ask students to look in their writing folders for a piece that they would like to revise for stronger word choice. Direct them to change some of the words or phrases in their piece, using the same techniques Fletcher did in *Hello, Harvest Moon*.

8. In partners, have students compare original words and phrases to their new words and phrases. Ask them to highlight their revised sections and tuck their pieces away for more work later.

FOLLOW UP:

- Read aloud Ralph Fletcher's *Twilight Comes Twice*. Have students call out words and phrases they like.
- Compare the phrases they liked in this book to those in *Hello, Harvest Moon*. What is similar? What is different?
- Discuss how words create voice and help readers identify an author's style.

Picture Books for Expanding Word Choice

More Than Anything Else

Marie Bradby, Author

Chris K. Soentpiet, Illustrator

Scholastic, 1995

The power of reading is the spotlight on this fictionalized account of the life of Booker T. Washington. Bradby gives students a look into the life of this famous American by vividly describing his life, his everyday world, and his intense desire, "more than anything else," to learn to read. The imagery in this piece is very strong; beautiful everyday language is used extremely well. The story has the powerful effect to lift the reader up and inspire each of us to appreciate the awesome role that literacy has in our lives.

Hello, Harvest Moon

Ralph Fletcher, Author

Kate Kiesler, Illustrator

Houghton Mifflin, 2003

A stunning complimentary piece to Fletcher's picture book *Twilight Comes Twice*, this delicious word feast is full of images and phrases that will bring readers great delight. The quiet elegance and simplicity of this work are just flat-out remarkable. Ralph Fletcher's beautiful language coupled with Kate Keilser's illustrations draw you in and let you marinate in the sights and sensations of the harvest moon. Every phrase takes you deeper into the experience: "With silent slippers it climbs the night stair, lifting free of the treetops to start working its magic, staining earth and sky with a ghostly glow." See focus lesson on page 85.

Miss Alaineus: A Vocabulary Disaster

Debra Frasier, Author and Illustrator

Harcourt, 2000

There's no question about which trait this book applies to—the key players are the words themselves. The language is playful, but at the same time there's a serious subtext about the pressure students feel when they're learning vocabulary. Sage, the main character, places a great deal of importance on the learning of isolated vocabulary words. Is this really how we want our students to learn about the majesty of words? There's an important lesson here for teachers and students.

Lincoln: A Photobiography
Russell Freedman, Author
Clarion, 1987

"Abraham Lincoln wasn't the sort of man who could lose himself in a crowd. After all, he stood six feet four inches tall, and, to top it off, he wore a high silk hat. His height was mostly in his long bony legs. When he sat in a chair, he seemed no taller than anyone else. It was only when he stood up that he towered above others."

This book teaches us that good descriptions not only come in words such as those above, but also in photographs. Freedman uses photographs to enhance our understanding of the piece. With words and pictures together, we really get it.

My Mama Had a Dancing Heart
Libba Moore Gray, Author
Raul Colon, Illustrator
Scholastic, 1999

"We'd dance a frog-hopping leaf-growing flower-opening hello spring ballet." This book is a word choice feast. A celebration of the relationship of a mother and daughter, the book flows from page to page with lyrical language, sparkling imagery, and words and phrases that feel good to say aloud. This book features outstanding word choice as well.

The Wolf Who Cried Boy
Bob Hartman, Author
Tim Raglin, Illustrator
Putnam Juvenile, 2002

Boy Chops? Baked Boy-tato? Boys-n-Berry Pie? The words in this piece are the focus for the retelling of a favorite old story written with a whole new spin. In this version, the wolf cries "boy" once too often, so when "boy" scouts—dozens of them—come into his family's cave, the wolf parents don't pay any attention. The plays on words in this story are a stitch. See focus lesson on page 98.

A Story for Bear
Dennis Haseley, Author
Jim LaMarche, Illustrator
Harcourt, 2002

The hardest thing about writing this annotation was figuring out which chapter to put it in. I especially love the language in this book. The carefully chosen words bring the text, about a young girl and a bear, to life. The girl reads to the bear in voices to match the type of story—scary, funny, lighthearted, and so on. The bear loves the stories, is magnetized by their magic, and yearns to be able to read for himself. The ending will make you cry. This is a lovely, lovely book.

Juan Verdades: The Man Who Couldn't Tell a Lie

Joe Hayes, Author
Joseph Daniel Fiedler, Illustrator
Orchard Books, 2001

English and Spanish come together in this familiar folk tale. So sure is don Ignacio that Juan will never tell a lie, he bets his entire ranch on it. Thanks to some clever word play, don Ignacio doesn't lose his ranch, but does find a man of honor, don Arturo, to marry his daughter. The author weaves together many cultures, rich language, and up-to-date, believable characters to create a memorable story.

Calling the Doves: El canto de las palomas

Juan Felipe Herrera, Author
Elly Simmons, Illustrator
Children's Book Press, 1995

Exquisite descriptions, written in both English and Spanish, celebrate the everyday life of a migrant farm worker. The close connection between the land and the lives of the people who work it are captured in lyrical prose. "Our dirt patio was a sand-colored theater where I learned to sing." And sing this book does. You will be drawn by its language and descriptions, which honor people whose lives have not always been easy, but who certainly lived with great honor and dignity.

Under the Quilt of Night

Deborah Hopkinson, Author
James E. Ransome, Illustrator
Atheneum Books, 2002

The author of the beloved *Sweet Clara and the Freedom Quilt* strikes a chord with this equally powerful book about the Underground Railroad. This story of a young black girl who is running from slavery glides through her escape with rhythm and grace that will leave you breathless. The author's careful choice of words creates tension and energy, and is sure to inspire students to look at choices in their own writing. Listen to this: "Freedom! I take a deep breath and when I let go my voice flies up in a song. My own song of running in sunshine and dancing through fields. I'll jump every fence in my way." Simple elegance. See focus lesson on page 102.

Armadillo Tattletale

Helen Ketteman, Author

Keith Graves, Illustrator

Scholastic, 2000

By definition, a tall tale stretches our imaginations because the author relies heavily on extravagant uses of words to engage the reader and create wonderful pictures of larger-than-life characters and places. Here is a tale of an armadillo that stretches the truth and learns how quickly that can get him into trouble. Much of it is clever, but all of it is excellent for word choice enthusiasts.

Walter the Farting Dog

William Kotzwinkle and Glenn Murray, Authors

Audrey Colman, Illustrator

Frog Ltd., 2001

Go ahead. Try and read this book to anyone—child or adult—and get through it without breaking down into side-splitting laughter. The book is illustrated with intricate collage that captures poor Walter's predicament—"he just farts morning, noon, and night." Readers will love the different ways the family tries to solve Walter's problem so they won't have to give him away. Walter saves the day, of course, and earns his place in the family, but not before some hilarious episodes. This book was a surprise find—and a must-have.

The Night I Followed the Dog

Nina Laden, Author and Illustrator

Chronicle Books, 1994

Posing the question, "It's 10 P.M. . . . Do you know where your dog is?" Ms. Laden pulls off a tour de force in this book. She uses active verbs and specific nouns throughout the text and illustrates a few nouns as she goes. For example, the word *limousine* is drawn as an actual limousine with the letters inside. From the first page, you can't help but focus on the clever use of the vocabulary coupled with the ingenious presentation.

Roberto the Insect Architect

Nina Laden, Author and Illustrator

Chronicle Books, 2000

Ms. Laden's books are rapidly becoming my favorites to use with students to point out and celebrate good word choice. They are clever, original, and extremely insightful. Every page brings new surprises and smiles as Roberto finds his way in life as an insect architect who builds unique structures for insect families who need them.

Cloud Dance

Thomas Locker, Author and Illustrator

Voyager Books, 2000

There is such beauty in this book. Listen to these words: "Nighttime clouds with silver edges shimmer in the moonlight." Isn't that just amazing? So visual. *Cloud Dance* is a blend of history, art, science, and sheer magic. The author chooses words so carefully and paints images so clearly, you can reach right out and touch them. This is a majestic, beautiful, and wondrous book. Other books to treasure by Thomas Locker include *Mountain Dance* and *Water Dance*.

Mirandy and Brother Wind

Patricia C. McKissack, Author

Jerry Pinkey, Illustrator

Alfred A. Knopf, 1988

Sparkling with life, this tale of life about forty years after the official end of slavery sweeps you away with its words and images. It is about a young girl's anticipation of her first cakewalk. Focusing on this historic period, the author uses a blend of African-American vernacular language of the time and lyrical everyday language. It's a beautiful piece that should be in every teacher's classroom.

Mama Will Be Home Soon

Nancy Minchella, Author

Keiko Narahashi, Illustrator

Scholastic, 2003

There is a simple elegance to this story. When Lili's mama goes away, Lili struggles with the loneliness that only a child can feel when separated from a parent. Lili looks for her mother everywhere, from the park to the beach, keeping a sharp eye out for the yellow hat that her mother promised to wear upon her return. Lili thinks she spots it in lots of places, but finally, when she begins to think she won't ever see her mother again, there it is—the yellow hat, and a hug to go with it. This is an example of beautiful, everyday language used very, very well.

Who's Got Game? The Ant or the Grasshopper?

Toni Morrison and Slade Morrison, Authors

Pascal Lemaitre, Illustrator

Scribner, 2003

This classic Aesop fable is told through the eyes of street-savvy kids—using and learning the language they know best. "How can you say I never worked a day? Art is work. It just looks like play." Told in rhyme and in wonderful cartoonlike drawings, this book brings new life to an age-old story. Toni Morrison is a gifted author who shares her love of words with readers and writers of all ages in this book co-authored with Slade Morrison.

Lauren McGill's Pickle Museum

Jerdine Nolen, Author

Debbie Tilley, Illustrator

Harcourt, 2003

Lauren just loves pickles. When she goes on a class field trip and an experiment goes wrong, she saves the day—and spreads her passion for pickles to the rest of the class. This make-you-smile book delights the reader and tickles the tongue with interesting words. Powerful verbs and precise nouns and modifiers are present on every page.

A Place to Grow

Soyung Pak, Author

Marcelino Truong, Illustrator

Scholastic, 2002

A family is like a seed. It needs a good, safe place to grow. So begins a father's explanation of his family's move from South Korea to America. The language in this book is rich with similes and metaphors and creates powerful images of the earth, life, and change. It's a gently told piece that teaches respect for a culture that may be unfamiliar to many readers.

Piggie Pie!

Margie Palatini, Author

Howard Fine, Illustrator

Houghton Mifflin, 1995

This is a book that will make you howl with laughter. Margie Palatini tells the story of a bigger-than-life witch and her search for something truly delicious to eat. The hardest part of working with this book will be deciding which trait you want to focus on. I choose word choice because it is so rich in nouns, verbs, and adjectives that really work. But sentence fluency, voice, ideas, and even organization are potentials for this text, too.

Dog Breath

Dav Pilkey, Author and Illustrator

Scholastic, 1994

Throughout this simple yet wonderful book, the author plays upon the word halitosis, the official name for bad breath. Pilkey, however, turns it into a main character, Hally, the Tosis family dog. As the family goes about trying to find ways to cure Hally's horrible breath, the writer continues to play with the original word. There are no single striking phrases here, just good clear writing. Pilkey frames the Hally Tosis name with text that supports it, but does not overwhelm it.

Into the A, B, Sea

Deborah Lee Rose, Author

Steve Jenkins, Illustrator

Scholastic, 2000

The alphabet book is a popular form of picture book—and a natural for word choice. In this example, we are delighted and informed at the same time. The author has taken great care to choose words carefully and accurately to create vivid pictures of beautiful sea creatures. At the end, she includes further information about all the creatures mentioned. Students should try their own A,B,C books for research projects and reports on other topics.

Epossumondas

Coleen Salley, Author

Janet Stevens, Illustrator

Harcourt, 2002

You better be careful what you say because Epossumondas might bring you something you really don't want and deliver it a way that may surprise you. Epossumondas is "the silliest, most loveable, most muddleheaded possum south of the Mason-Dixon line." This lively little story is sure to delight readers with the literal way Epossumondas carries out his sweet Auntie's directions of how to carry butter and how to hold a dog. This is the perfect book to use to teach students the importance of being accurate and precise with words.

Noodle Man

April Pulley Sayre, Author

Stephen Costanza, Illustrator

Scholastic, 2002

"Al Dente was born into a pasta-loving family." Get it? The plays on words and the references to all things pasta make this book a fun read. Business isn't going so well for the Dente family. Most people seem to be ordering pizzas, which don't bring in nearly as much money as entrees. That is, of course, until pasta turns out to be the key to saving children, catching the bad guys, and making everyone's life a little better. In addition to Sayre's amusing word choices, her voice is light and humorous, too. The pages fly by.

Baloney (Henry P.)

Jon Scieszka, Author

Lane Smith, Illustrator

Penguin Putnam, 2001

If you love to play with words, *Baloney (Henry P.)* is just the book for you. This book appears to use a lot of nonsense words—words that I had never heard before, certainly. It isn't all that hard to figure out what they mean, however, because Scieszka and Smith put them in a helpful—and hilarious—context. The story is wonderful, right up until the end when the reader discovers that the "nonsense" words are actually real words from obscure languages. Absorbing all the information on the chart at the back of the book is a powerful eye-opener on word choice all by itself. See focus lesson on page 104.

Food Fight!

Carol Diggory Shields, Author

Doreen Gay-Kassel, Illustrator

Handprint Books, 2002

Readers will delight to find out what happens in the kitchen at night. As the food comes to life and emerges from the refrigerator, the cupboards, and the cabinets, there is a rocking good time. "'Lettuce have a party,' said the salad greens. And they slid to the floor on a bunch of string beans." A playfulness with language runs through this cute and original story—words that delight and surprise the reader.

Raising Sweetness

Diane Stanley, Author

Brian Karas, Illustrator

G.P. Putnam's Sons, 1999

This is a book that will warm any English teacher's heart. It is based on the premise that learning to write is as essential as learning to read, and how both processes support one another. It's clever, funny, original, and the words rock and roll through the piece. Here's how it starts: "It was just another regular day in Possum Trot. I was sittin' at the kitchen table, trying to figure out what to rustle up for dinner. I thought about pot roast, but I was plumb out of syrup." With all the peculiar sayings in this book, the voice pops right out. Add this liveliness to the important message about literacy and you have the ingredients of a surefire hit.

Brave Potatoes

Toby Speed, Author

Barry Root, Illustrator

G.P. Putnam's Sons, 2000

This book is lively, fresh, original, and sure to delight the reader. I found myself laughing out loud as I read this story of prize-winning potatoes that try to outwit Hickemup the Chef at the county fair. It seems that Hickemup has all the ingredients for his tasty stew, except for potatoes. And those potatoes aren't about to be chopped up by the likes of him. So late one night the potatoes and their vegetable allies have an all-out showdown with the chef. Filled with interesting and action-packed words, readers will enjoy every page of this clever story. See focus lesson on page 101.

Subway Sparrow

Leyla Torres, Author and Illustrator

Farrar, Straus and Giroux, 1993

A small sparrow flies into a subway car and is trapped, forcing communication between people who normally ride the subway in complete silence. As they learn to work together to save the sparrow, the passengers develop an understanding and appreciation for the very human need to communicate—no matter what language we speak.

The Starry Night

Neil Waldman, Author and Illustrator

Boyds Mills Press, 1999

Vincent van Gogh has long been one of my favorite artists. He used paint the way great writers use words—to evoke sensations and feelings you didn't even realize were there. In this imaginative and colorful text, young Bernard is fascinated by a man painting in the park. The pictures give you clues that it is Vincent Van Gogh, but the words don't. Instead, they create a sense of wonder and mystery about the chance encounter between these two. Bernard takes Vincent on a tour of his beloved New York City, and Vincent continues to paint. When it is time for Vincent to go, he leads Bernard to one of his most famous paintings, *Starry Night*, and disappears. Saddened and feeling abandoned, Bernard finds comfort by beginning a painting of his own.

Bullfrog Pops!

Rick Walton, Author

Chris McAllister, Illustrator

Gibbs Smith, 1999

The town of Ravenous Gulch will never be the same now that Bullfrog has arrived on the scene. So hungry that he devours everything in sight, Bullfrog takes off and gets everyone he meets in an uproar as the story unfolds. What makes this book especially fun to use is that each page ends with an active verb, which prompts students to stop and predict what will come next. But the verb always leads them to a place they didn't expect, so prepare for some surprises along the way. What better way to teach students the power of active verbs than through Bullfrog's hilarious escapades? See focus lesson on page 99.

Once There Was a Bull . . . (frog)

Rick Walton, Author

Greg Hally, Illustrator

The Putnam & Grosset Group, 1995

What's a bullfrog to do when he loses his hop? This book is about just that. Bullfrog looks everywhere for his hop! Walton teases us with his word choice. On every other page, he invites the reader to guess the last word. Examples: "He landed in a patch of grass . . ." "hoppers." and "'I'll do it,' said a cow . . ." "boy." Students have a great time predicting. Teach your students the fun of compound words with this entertaining story!

Why the Banana Split

Rick Walton, Author

Jimmy Holder, Illustrator

Gibbs Smith, 1998

If there is one author to lock onto to help teach students how to use powerful and delightful verbs in their writing, Rick Walton is it! He uses hilarious language to describe how characters run away from a scary-looking dinosaur named Rex: "The jump ropes skipped town," "The basketball players went traveling, while the baseball players struck out on their own," "The jackhammers hit the road," "The lettuce headed out." Fabulous. Word choice is this author's forte!

The Adventures of Jules & Gertie

Esther Pearl Watson, Author and Illustrator

Harcourt, 1999

Watson uses a combination of literary devices such as metaphors and similes to create her unique voice in this piece. The reader delights in passages such as: "She felt lonely as an echo. Her best friend was gone, and those greasy outlaws would drop her into a pit of squirming rattlers if she stopped dancing." Read and enjoy. Sometimes it's just plain fun to read a piece by an author who uses words so deliciously.

Henny-Penny

Jane Wattenberg, Author and Illustrator

Scholastic, 2000

The sky might be falling once again, but never has the event been told with more energy. Listen to this opening: "Stormy skies and whirling winds flip-flapped around the barnyard. Henny-Penny scratched about for a tasty bite to each when . . .WHACK! An acorn smacked Henny-Penny right on top of her fine red comb." Filled with life and sparkle, this version of the familiar tale will fascinate and surprise readers . . . and inspire writers.

Miz Berlin Walks

Jane Yolen, Author

Floyd Cooper, Illustrator

Puffin Books, 1997

Everyday words and phrases used exquisitely are the hallmark of this enchanting story of an older woman and her friendship with a younger girl. As the two characters come to know one another during walks in the neighborhood, the reader is treated to lyrical prose that describes events in their lives: ". . . the hurricane of '48, when water lapped like wet tongues at the front steps of houses all the way to Kecoughtan Road and trees were bent near double."

Focus Lessons for Expanding Word Choice

Focus Lesson Based On . . .

The Wolf Who Cried Boy
Bob Hartman, Author
Tim Raglin, Illustrator
Putnam Juvenile, 2002
(See description on page 88.)

Target Trait: Word Choice
Secondary Traits: Ideas, Voice, Organization

Materials:

- A copy of *The Wolf Who Cried Boy*
- Chart of foods from *The Wolf Who Cried Boy* (See chart at right.)
- Chart paper and markers
- Writing paper and pens or pencils
- Boys-n-berry Pie Recipe on a piece of chart paper

Favorite Recipes from *The Wolf Who Cried Boy:*

Lamburgers	Boys-n-Berry Pie
Sloppy Does	Three-Pig Salad
Chocolate Moose	Chipmunks and Dip
Boy Chops	Granny Smith Pie
Baked Boy-tato	Muskratatouille

In this hilarious story, *The Wolf Who Cried Boy*, students experience a new twist on an old tale. With this lesson, students experiment with different choices of words by designing a "cookbook" of some of the little wolf's favorite boy recipes.

What to Do:

1. Read *The Wolf Who Cried Boy* aloud to the class.
2. Ask students to refer to the chart of the foods that are mentioned in the story.
3. Put students into small groups of three or four, and have them come up with four additional "boy" dishes. Have the groups share aloud the dishes they came up with. List the names of the dishes on the chart paper as they are described.

4. Make copies of the Boys-n-berry Pie with Fried Chipmunk Crust recipe and hand out one to every student along with paper and pencils or pens. Discuss the elements of a successful recipe such as a list of the specific ingredients, quantities, and a step-by-step set of directions.

5. In small groups, ask students to write two "boy" recipes using as much creative language as possible while being clear and well-organized.

**Example:
Boys-n-berry Pie with Fried Chipmunk Crust**

1 boy (plucked eyebrows)

3 cups fresh berries (ask your bear friends where the best berries are)

1 cup of honey (be careful of bee stings . . . bear friends should warn you of this)

1 pie crust (made from leftover fried chipmunk)

Take your boy and pluck his eyebrows so there will be no stray eyebrow hairs in your pie. In a bowl, mix him together with your fresh berries and honey. Be careful to make sure to stir all ingredients completely.

In another bowl, take your leftover fried chipmunk and crush into a fine powder. Firmly pat into the bottom of a pie plate.

Pour your boys-n-berry mixture over your fried chipmunk crust and bake in 350 degree oven for 1 hour.

Remove from oven and let cool. Serve with a dollop of Chocolate Moose.

Follow Up:

- Create a new list of foods with animals' names in them and try writing some new recipes.
- Assemble a completed cookbook to add to the classroom library.

Focus Lesson Based On . . .

Bullfrog Pops!
Rick Walton, Author
Chris McAllister, Illustrator
Gibbs Smith, 1999
(See description on page 96.)

Target Trait: Word Choice
Secondary Traits: Ideas, Voice

The power of verbs is never more evident than in this delightful story about a bullfrog that hops into Ravenous Gulch in search of food. In *Bullfrog Pops!* each page ends with an active verb that leads to a twist in the story on the next page.

MATERIALS:

- A copy of *Bullfrog Pops!*
- Writing paper and pens or pencils

WHAT TO DO:

1. Discuss the use of active verbs versus passive verbs with the class. With an active verb, the subject of the sentence is doing something: "Carmen thumped the melon to see if it was ripe." With a passive verb, something is being done *to* the subject. "The melon was thumped by Carmen to see if it was ripe." Emphasize to students that active verbs add energy to writing, whereas passive verbs tend to weigh it down.

2. Read *Bullfrog Pops!* aloud. At the end of each page, stop and ask students to predict what happens next and call out their ideas. For example, the first page reads: "Once there was a bullfrog who hopped. . . ." Students may call out: "over the lily pad," "across the town," "fast," or "on one leg."

3. Turn the page and read what Walton wrote: "a stagecoach." Continue reading to the end of the next page, which also ends with a strong verb, and ask students to predict what comes next. Continue this process until you reach the end.

4. After finishing the reading, ask students if they were surprised at some of the turns the story took. How does Walton create a story with these surprises? How important is the verb to his technique?

5. Ask students to go back to the story and find a place where they could add a new page that ends in an active verb, without changing the main story line. Allow time for them to write and illustrate their new pages and insert them into the original text.

6. Read the story with the new pages. Note how students used verbs to duplicate Walton's technique.

FOLLOW UP:

- Have the students write and illustrate another story about Bullfrog. Can they surprise the reader with what happens next by using an active verb at the end of each page?
- Create a list of active verbs to display in the classroom. Encourage students to add to it as they find good examples from texts.

Focus Lesson Based On . . .

Brave Potatoes
Toby Speed, Author
Barry Root, Illustrator
G.P. Putnam's Sons, 2000
(See description on page 95.)

Target Trait: Word Choice
Secondary Traits: Voice, Presentation

With this lesson, students learn fresh and unusual ways to use words that appeal to the senses. As they hear Speed's excellent use of words to move the story forward, they will want to try using more specific and interesting words in their own pieces.

Materials:

- A copy of *Brave Potatoes*
- A potato for every student
- Overhead transparencies and markers
- Writing paper and pens or pencils

What to Do:

1. Give every student a raw potato. (A ten-pound bag of russets contains about thirty.) As a class, brainstorm words to describe potatoes—*brown*, *rough*, *hard*, *dusty*—and list them on the overhead transparency.

2. Write the sensory words *see*, *touch*, *hear*, *taste*, and *smell* on the overhead and ask students to list words about potatoes under each sensory word category. For example, they might put *crusty* and *bumpy* under *touch*; and *musty* and *dirty* under *smell.*

3. On another transparency, write the following words from the book: *brave*, *prize*, *rolling*, *wide-awake*, *fearless*, *aviating*, *wee buds*, *mesmerizing*, *death-defying*, *spinning*, and *chef-defying*. Ask students: "Can you imagine using these words to describe potatoes?"

4. Read *Brave Potatoes* aloud. Ask students to listen for these words and phrases, and decide if they like the language. After reading, discuss students' reactions to the words.

5. Ask students to write their own stories about a potato, using the real potato sitting on their desks to spark their imagination. Use these questions to get them started:
   - Who is your story about?
   - What is your main character's problem?
   - How will this problem be resolved?

Here is what one third grader wrote:

Bud is an Idaho russet potato who lives in a potato patch near Idaho Falls, Idaho. He is three months old, four inches long and as big around as a tennis ball. His mother brags that he is a perfect, dirty brown color with beautiful, rough skin, and some day he will be mashed as creamy white as milk and lie beside roast beef and peas while yummy mushroom gravy drips down his sides. This sounds perfect for a potato, but Bud has a problem; he doesn't want to be mashed potatoes on a plate. That sounds too much like old potato thinking. Bud sees the fast-food restaurant trucks drive by on the highway every day, and that's where he wants to end up, as crispy, salty, crunchy French fries side by side with a big, juicy cheeseburger. He wants to tell his mother, but he just can't find the courage.

Focus Lesson Based On . . .

Under the Quilt of Night

Deborah Hopkinson, Author

James E. Ransome, Illustrator

Atheneum Books, 2002

(See description on page 89.)

Target Trait: Word Choice

Secondary Traits: Voice, Ideas

Through this captivating picture book, students examine the use of strong verbs to make writing powerful and memorable. Specifically, they create a newspaper story about the book, using some of their favorite verbs from the book. They also get the opportunity to connect the written word to art since the author uses images of quilts to add details to the story.

MATERIALS:

- Six copies of *Under the Quilt of Night*
- A list of all the chapter titles from the book to distribute to students
- Butcher paper divided into 12 squares, 6-by-6 inches each (three squares across, four down)
- Writing paper, pencils, crayons, and markers

WHAT TO DO:

1. Show students the cover of the book and ask them to predict what it is about. Then ask them what they know about the Underground Railroad. (There is a very good section at the back of the book called "Note About the Story" for background information.)

2. Walk students through the book, showing them each chapter and its title. Ask them to consider what each title means. Point out that each title is an *ing* verb: *running*, *waiting*, *watching*, *hiding*, *traveling*, and *singing*. Ask if using a verb in a title is effective. What is the author trying to convey to the reader by using these verbs for titles?

3. Read *Under the Quilt of Night* to the class.

4. Break the class into six groups. Assign each group a chapter from the book. Have each group:
    - Read its chapter aloud together (choral reading)
    - Pick out strong, energetic verbs and list them on a piece of paper (For example, *pounding*, *hoeing*, *mending*, *fence*, and *crouch*.)
    - Share lists with the class

5. As a class, choose 12 verbs that are the most strong and energetic from the group lists. Be sure to discuss with students why they are selecting certain words over others. List these words on the individual squares of the butcher paper to make a word quilt.

6. Ask groups to write book reviews that explain how *Under the Quilt of Night* got its title, including as many verbs from the word quilt as possible. Encourage students to use other interesting words as well.

FOLLOW UP:

- Read page 3, focusing on the line ". . . my feet make drumbeats." Discuss what the author means and ask students to draw their interpretations.
- Have each student choose a descriptive phrase from the book, such as "My breath is gone," and "I pull the darkness around me, under the quilt of night." Then have them draw a picture to illustrate what it means.

Focus Lesson Based On . . .

Baloney (Henry P.)

Jon Scieszka, Author
Lane Smith, Illustrator
Penguin Putnam, 2001
(See description on page 94.)

Target Trait: Word Choice
Secondary Traits: Voice, Ideas

This amazing duo is at it again. Like Scieszka and Smith's past collaborations, *Baloney (Henry P.)* is witty, clever, original, and able to teach us a great deal about words and phrases.

Materials:

- A copy of *Baloney (Henry P.)*
- Overhead transparencies and markers
- Writing paper and pens or pencils

What to Do:

1. Read the book aloud to students in a lively fashion. However, *don't* read the last two pages, which contain the "Decoder Page"—an answer key, of sorts. Let the students think that the words are silly and made up.

2. Ask students to make a list of words from *Baloney (Henry P.)* they don't recognize, such as Zimulus, fracasse, aamu, and sighing flosser, and record them on the overhead.

3. Read the book again. This time, ask students to raise their hands when they hear an unfamiliar word and consider what it could mean from its context. Ask for a volunteer to write a definition next to the word on the overhead.

4. Show students the Decoder Page at the end of the text. Share the list of words from this page, their definitions, and the places in the text where they appear. Compare Scieszka and Smith's definitions to the ones students made up.

Follow Up:

- Teach students what a palindrome is (a word that reads the same forward and backward). Have them write a few and try to add them to *Baloney (Henry P.)*.

CHAPTER FIVE

Developing Sentence Fluency

"Like fine poetry, children's picture books are meant to be seen and heard. Even adolescents like to be read to. . . . By reading aloud I not only let kids hear the richness of the language, but I invite adolescents to read them also."

—Linda Rief
Beyond Words: Picture Books for Older Readers and Writers

One of the best ways to teach writers how to create sentence fluency is by hearing beautiful language read aloud, and picture books are a perfect resource. They can be read in one sitting and, because each word and phrase has been examined, revised, moved, and scrutinized long and hard before publication, they serve as stellar models of rhythm and flow.

Poetry books are a natural fit, such as *Gathering the Sun* by Alma Flor Ada and *Hey You! C'mere: A Poetry Slam* by Elizabeth Swados. So are books that lend themselves to choral reading, such as *Bat Loves the Night* by Nicola Davies, *Dream Weaver* by Jonathan London, *Gauchada* by C. Drew Lamm, or *Dogteam* by Gary Paulsen. Although prose, these books use powerful rhythmic cadences that make choral readings a pleasure.

What follows is a list of the strongest books for sentence fluency that I have discovered in the past several years. You probably have access to books in your school media center, the public library, or your own personal collection that will work just as well. When you find a good one, make note of it on the cover or inside page. I put a green adhesive dot, available in most office supply stores, to indicate books for sentence fluency. I use other colors for the other traits. If a picture book is truly good, it can probably be used to cover several traits, but it's a good idea to note a target trait to simplify organization.

Sentence Fluency: A Definition

Sentence fluency is the auditory trait. We read with our ears as much as with our eyes. As we take in the words and phrases on the page, ideally, we hear a melody. As a result, we receive more meaning from the piece as we are drawn into its rhythm and flow. Sometimes the writer surprises us with a short declarative statement or a fragment. Sometimes she uses long sentences to marinate us in images. To capture what the writer has in mind, sentences must move beyond correctness and on to more treacherous ground. They must contain just the right phrase or word in just the right place to create just the right image. Here is a lesson based on a nonfiction text that is exceptionally fluent:

FEATURE FOCUS LESSON BASED ON . . .

Bat Loves the Night
Nicola Davies, Author
Sarah Fox-Davies, Illustrator
Candlewick Press, 2001
(See description on page 111.)

Target Trait: Sentence Fluency
Secondary Traits: Voice, Ideas

Nicola Davies describes a day in the life of bats in this musical and mellifluous book. As you read it aloud, students will hear the rhythms and cadences of carefully crafted writing. They will learn how two different modes of writing, descriptive and expository, can be combined in one text.

MATERIALS:

- A copy of *Bat Loves the Night* for every four to five students
- Index cards and pens or pencils

WHAT TO DO:

1. Give each student an index card. Ask them to write down everything they know or think they know about bats.

2. Walk students through *Bat Loves the Night*, showing them how Davies weaves together two different modes of writing, descriptive and expository.

3. Divide the class in half and assign each group to either the descriptive text or the expository text. Pass out the books.

4. Tell the groups that they are going to be reading their parts orally. Give students time to read and familiarize themselves with their sections.

5. Rehearse for the oral reading. Groups may decide to read some lines as a group, in pairs, or as single readers.

6. Encourage students to practice reading their parts several times, gauging how slow or fast to go, until they are satisfied with the flow.

7. To stage the oral reading, arrange each group of students in a circle. The descriptive text group forms an inside circle facing out; the expository text group makes an outside circle facing in.

8. Let both groups practice reading their texts, according to their plan, adding movements to enrich the final presentation.

9. Have students perform their reading of *Bat Loves the Night* from beginning to end. Afterward, discuss how their plan for the reading worked. If time is available, let students read the text again.

10. Have students look back at the index card they filled out at the beginning of the lesson and add information they learned about bats.

FOLLOW UP:

- Invite students to read other books by Davies and discuss the sentence fluency in each book.
- Challenge students to use topics from science to write their own picture books in Davies's style, blending descriptive and expository together to make the writing flow.

Picture Books for Developing Sentence Fluency

Gathering the Sun

Alma Flor Ada, Author
Simon Silva, Illustrator
Lothrop, Lee & Shepard, 1994

This brilliant alphabet book contains short poems in Spanish and English that, collectively, depict how plants, fruits, vegetables, people, and feelings impact the lives of Hispanic agricultural workers. Filled with emotion and pride of a rich cultural heritage, this book gives voice to the experience of Hispanic farm workers. This is a text that begs to be read aloud; the poems flow through the alphabet and resonate deeply with the reader in Spanish and English.

Behold the Trees

Sue Alexander, Author
Leonid Gore, Illustrator
Scholastic, 2001

"Trees. Leaves, twigs, branches, bark-covered trunks, roots going down into dark, damp soil. Shields for the earth against the searing sun and drying winds." So begins this fascinating and beautifully written piece honoring trees of Israel and the thousands of years they have been on the earth. Enormously visual and poignant, this book teaches us how much is lost when we harvest the trees, but leaves the reader with the hope that the renewal cycle has begun.

Hide and Snake

Keith Baker, Author and Illustrator
Harcourt, 1991

Keith Baker's words are simple and exact. He weaves them together seamlessly, paying careful attention to where he wants his reader to focus. Baker is a master at doing a lot with a little. In this striking work, he uses a snake to weave the message together, one simple word or phrase at a time. It's not surprising that when students choose an icon or image to stand for sentence fluency, they often pick a snake; the way the snake moves like liquid across the hard soil is a good mental image to have when writing sentences. This book uses Baker's artistry and his own well-crafted sentences to make a connection to sentence fluency.

The Important Book

Margaret Wise Brown, Author

Leonard Weisgard, Illustrator

HarperCollins, 1999

This gem has been in print for over fifty years. It features poetry that is created using a pattern, repeating the first line as the last line of the poem. In the middle, the poems are made of different numbers of nicely phrased lines. But all the poems use the same bookend strategy by beginning and ending the poem with the same line. Any time you read or write poetry, you are working with sentence fluency as you listen for the rhythm and flow of the words and phrases. After reading a few of Brown's poems, you can follow her pattern to create your own *The Important Book* poems. The book is a good template for many different poem topics, such as the important thing about each of the traits, or the important thing that a student learned in school today. See focus lesson on page 120.

Night of the Gargoyles

Eve Bunting, Author

David Wiesner, Illustrator

Clarion Books, 1994

Bunting continues her string of wonderful books for children with this fascinating and richly illustrated text. This piece's language is particularly stunning—its light tempo and quick pulse describe the world of gargoyles. Every page holds new surprises as Bunting provides us with a text that has exquisite phrasing.

Goal

Robert Burleigh, Author

Stephen T. Johnson, Illustrator

Harcourt, 2001

My eyes lit up in delight when I saw this Robert Burleigh book at the bookstore. He never disappoints. This time his topic is the game of soccer, and like his earlier piece on basketball, entitled *Hoops*, Burleigh takes us right into the center of the sport. We feel every moment through the nuances of his fluency. It would be interesting to take these two pieces and look at the fluency techniques he uses to make each so extraordinary. Soccer fan or not, you'll enjoy reading this piece. The movement Burleigh creates is masterful.

Home Run

Robert Burleigh, Author

Mike Wimmer, Illustrator

Harcourt, 1998

Robert Burleigh is one of my favorite picture book authors. He has a way with words and phrases that knocks me out every time. The topics of his books are always those that you know your students will love, so getting the books into their hands will be a snap. Beyond that, though, he knows how to write with beauty and grace. Listen to this excerpt from *Home Run*: "Then there is only the echoey, nothing-quite-like-it sound and the soft feel of the fat part of the bat on the center of the ball. Babe understands this feeling. He does not know when or where, but he waits for it. Again and again." Sheer poetry. What a gift this author has. When teaching sentence fluency, make sure you have at least one Robert Burleigh text!

Hoops

Robert Burleigh, Author

Stephen T. Johnson, Illustrator

Harcourt Brace, 1997

You will love the way Robert Burleigh uses creative sentence fluency to help you experience the feeling of basketball. This book can model for students how they might try a one- or two-word sentence or a longer, flowing sentence.

Lookin' for Bird in the Big City

Robert Burleigh, Author

Marek Los, Illustrator

Harcourt, 2001

Another Burleigh direct hit. His use of language is so stellar, that I think I can safely say that any time you run across one of his titles, grab it. It will be a grand read, and a pleasure to use as a teaching aid.

Pandora

Robert Burleigh, Author

Raul Colon, Illustrator

Harcourt, 2002

This text, based on the Greek fable of Pandora and the Box, is an artful blend of prose and verse. A short reference page is provided with the names and attributes of the most noted of the Greek gods, and some background information sets the story in motion.

Bat Loves the Night

Nicola Davies, Author

Sarah Fox-Davies, Illustrator

Candlewick Press, 2001

I'm such a fan of Nicola Davies. Her information books always strike gold in my book. How bats live may be the subject of this book, but it is the contrasting styles of descriptive, almost poetic, text and fact-focused, expository text that just knocks me out. See focus lesson on page 106.

One Tiny Turtle

Nicola Davies, Author

Jane Chapman, Illustrator

Candlewick Press, 2001

Another perfect book by Nicola Davies. The blend of descriptive and expository modes, and the careful attention to every last syllable, make her books excellent read-alouds, and amazing models of how to write about science with energy, beauty, and voice. I love how she includes an index at the end of the picture book so the reader can go back and find out specific information about turtles. But mostly, I love how this book reads. Don't miss Davies' other books *Big Blue Whale* and *Wild About Dolphins*.

Why Butterflies Go By On Silent Wings

Marguerite W. Davol, Author

Robert Roth, Illustrator

Scholastic, 2001

This folk tale invites you into a world that existed before humans came along. It was noisy—all those creatures and bugs and flowers pulsing and alive with energy—but then one surprising day it became thunderous. During an intense lightning storm, the insects were thrown into the mud, and when they recovered, they noticed, for the first time, the beauty of their world. Enjoy this piece for its poetic melody and its sheer reverence for the natural world.

Twilight Comes Twice

Ralph Fletcher, Author

Kate Kiesler, Illustrator

Clarion Books, 1997

The sister book to Fletcher's latest, *Hello, Harvest Moon* (which is described in Chapter 4, Word Choice), this exquisite text is the kind of model we want students to read, savor, and imitate in their own way. Every syllable is carefully selected for just the right sound, creating a gentle rhythm. As you read, the images will linger in your mind long after you turn the last page. This quietly elegant text goes deep inside an ordinary event in an extraordinary way.

Harriet, You'll Drive Me Wild!

Mem Fox, Author

Marla Frazee, Illustrator

Harcourt, 2000

"Just like that." ". . . and she was." These two-line endings, which appear on each alternating page of this oh-so-true picture book, create a rhythm that rolls off your tongue. It is a perfectly crafted set of phrases and sentences. Mem is a master at this; her work is so satisfying to the ear. Try not to read this aloud. Go ahead, try.

Flicker Flash

Joan Bransfield Graham, Author

Nancy Davis, Illustrator

Houghton Mifflin, 1999

Ever inventive with language, Graham illuminates her ideas with smooth phrasing and a graceful fluidity in this collection of concrete poems. This is a nice book to share with students if you want them to listen to the sounds that are created when key words are placed in just the right places.

Come On, Rain!

Karen Hesse, Author

Jon J. Muth, Illustrator

Scholastic, 1999

Children will love the suspense that builds as Tessie and her friends await a rain shower and the joy they feel dancing in the long-awaited rain. Written as a lyrical piece of prose, your students will be able to hear how Hesse uses sentence structure to keep the action moving, rather than stopping the reader—much the way rain clouds constantly move across the sky.

Don't Take Your Snake for a Stroll

Karin Ireland, Author

David Catrow, Illustrator

Harcourt, 2003

As every pet owner knows, there are just some places you should not go with your pet, no matter how much you love it. In this funny story, you will find out that rhinos shouldn't go dancing, pigs aren't made for shopping, and allowing chimps to hang from holiday lights leads to nothing but disaster. As you read, you and your students will find yourselves caught up in the rhythm and rhyme of each page. Encourage students to try Ireland's pattern in their own writing. Let them think of other animals and places where they wouldn't take them because of their natural behaviors and physical characteristics.

Bad Dog

Nina Laden, Author and Illustrator

Walker & Company, 2000

Without a doubt, this book is a perfect fit for word choice and sentence fluency. But because I have listed a couple of other Nina Laden books under word choice, let's look at this one a bit differently. This book has great sentences—flashy and brilliant with that "just right" feel. Laden begins, "So they say I'm a bad dog. I know I'm no Saint Bernard, but it's not like I robbed a bank of anything." She moves on to, "I was bored. Running on empty. Empty water dish, empty food bowl. So I emptied the trash can. That's when I found it. My inspiration." The careful combination of chopped phrases and long sentences makes this book a good one to study for sentence fluency.

Gauchada

C. Drew Lamm, Author

Fabian Negrin, Illustrator

Alfred A. Knopf, 2002

Thanks to Dr. Jim Blasingame for recommending *Gauchada*, which is written so well that it reads like free-verse poetry. Filled with images and words that will enchant readers and teach them a bit about life on the pampas in Argentina, this book will be one you return to over and over. The lilt of the sentences, coupled with the naturalness of the phrasing, create sentence fluency that just melts in your mouth as you read this story aloud.

John Henry

Julius Lester, Author

Jerry Pinkney, Illustrator

Puffin Books, 1994

This retelling of the classic heroic tale of the human spirit contains powerful imagery and carefully chosen words and phrases, making it a fine piece to examine for sentence fluency. You'll also love it for its humor and compassion. Try reading this version to students and then reading an earlier version. Which one is stronger in each of the traits? Lester's version scores high on sentence fluency, word choice, and voice. See focus lesson on page 122.

Dream Weaver

Jonathan London, Author

Rocco Baviera, Illustrator

Harcourt, 1998

Spider magic! Students will enjoy the rhythms and sounds of the carefully chosen words as they roll off the tongue. Use this piece for choral reading—it's a perfect example of how beautiful prose should sound. Notice, too, that there is a page in the back containing spider facts, to provide the background information for students to appreciate this book to the fullest. See focus lesson on page 119.

My Name Is Jorge: On Both Sides of the River

Jane Medina, Author

Fabricio Vanden Broeck, Illustrator

Boyds Mills Press, 1999

Through poems in English and Spanish, we meet Jorge, a young boy who is struggling to embrace the United States, the country into which he has been adopted, but not forget his homeland, Mexico. This book allows the reader to hear the words and phrases in two different languages. The result is an eloquent and graceful book.

A Snowman Named Just Bob

Mark Kimball Moulton, Author

Karen Hillard Crouch, Illustrator

Lang Books, 1999

Written in rhyme, this magical story of a snowman reminds us all of the value of true friendship. "Friendship is a simple thing, the clue is just to start. As long as it is built on trust, and love from in your heart." So goes the story of a simple snowman named Bob. The language in this text is graceful and delicate. The flow of the words leads you gently, page by page, to a satisfying conclusion.

Black Cat

Christopher Myers, Author and Illustrator

Scholastic, 1999

Follow the trail of the black cat as he streaks through the streets of the city, "ducking under the red circling of sirens cutting through the night," "chasing subway mice and platform rats," "seeking sun-soaked spots on hot tar beaches," off into the night. This poem is a splendid example of how a piece's sentence fluency creates voice. Every syllable is carefully timed; every line is in perfect rhythm with the next.

The Web Files

Margie Palatini, Author

Richard Egielski, Illustrator

Hyperion Books, 2001

This book screams sentence fluency and word choice. From the line "Someone has pilfered a peck of perfect purple almost-pickled peppers," we are sent on a captivating, mystery-solving adventure. But it's not only the language choices that make this piece stand out. Ellipses, hyphens, dashes, and a full range of other punctuation marks draw you into the text and create the energy and flow of the piece. The story is written in a detective genre style; the facts ma'am, nothing but the facts. Short chopped sentences with alliteration to tie your tongue over make this a favorite text. See focus lesson on page 118.

All By Herself

Ann Whitford Paul, Author

Michael Steirnagle, Illustrator

Harcourt, 1999

The fourteen girls featured in this book went on to become women of great accomplishments—from Rachel Carson to Wanda Gag to Wilma Rudolph. Through poems about them, you learn about their motivations. By sharing the poems with students, you bring home the point that no matter who or where you are, you can make a difference. The poems are varied and written in a way that is perfectly suited to the different personalities and histories of each woman.

Dogteam

Gary Paulsen, Author

Ruth Wright Paulsen, Illustrator

Dragonfly, 1995

Close your eyes and try to imagine the feeling of driving a dog sled on a cold, crisp, clear night. Gary Paulsen recreates this image through the rhythm and cadence of his writing. "Through the trees, in and out, the sled whipping after them, through the trees with no sound but the song of the runners, the high-soft-shusshh-whine of the runners." When students hear this book read aloud, they will feel themselves being whisked through the snow right along with the author.

Our Family Tree: An Evolution Story

Lisa Westberg Peters, Author

Lauren Stringer, Illustrator

Harcourt, 2003

"But then the earth changed. Land rose from the oceans. The air filled with oxygen. Life changed, too." This is just a taste of the lovely prose in this book intended to intrigue, inform, and delight readers as they learn about evolution. Peters's placement of the words and phrases is musical—poetry. Its rhythms and beats beg to be read aloud. *Our Family Tree* is an excellent candidate for choral reading. Add it to your collection of beautifully written content books.

Oh, the Places You'll Go!

Dr. Seuss, Author and Illustrator

Random House, 1990

It seems clichéd to include Dr. Seuss under sentence fluency because we all know what a master of the trait he was, but this piece is special and one you should have in your classroom. It reads with a smoothness that shows attention to every syllable and sound in every word. It's a wise and wonderful tale filled with long and short sentences and delightful surprises on every page. Success is within every person's grasp. That's the central message of this book. Could there be a better one to share with students over and over again?

Two Cool Cows

Toby Speed, Author

Barry Root, Illustrator

Putnam, 1995

One look at this book's whimsical cover of two cool cows, complete with shades, and you'll know you are in for a romp. The cows swing through familiar nursery rhymes with energy and bounce, never missing a beat. The text reads like free verse poetry in some places, rhyming text in others, and has tons of terrific tongue twisters.

Hey You! C'mere: A Poetry Slam

Elizabeth Swados, Author

Joe Cepeda, Illustrator

Scholastic, 2002

You and your students will find yourselves tapping your toes and drumming your fingers to the different rhythms and beats of the fourteen poems in this collection. The poems capture the sights and sounds of a neighborhood on a summer day. The universal joys and struggles of daily life echo from these poems. It's a slam, an event in which poets perform their work and are judged by members of the audience, so you may want to have students perform these poems and then vote on their favorites. See focus lesson on page 123.

Sebastian: A Book About Bach

Jeanette Winter, Author and Illustrator

Harcourt, 1999

There is a strong connection between sentence fluency and music, and this book is living proof. The book, written with an easy fluidity, will transport readers to a time when music was the entertainment of the evening, not TV. As the story of Bach unfolds, you and your students will gain an appreciation of his genius and ability to create compositions that make the world a richer, more brilliant place.

Tough Cookie

David Wisniewski, Author and Illustrator

Lothrop, Lee & Shepard, 1999

Wisniewski spins a wildly imaginative tale about the trials and tribulations of life as a cookie in a cookie jar using the clipped, staccato style of the detective genre. It's the perfect book to teach students about writing. You can focus on Wisniewski's voice, which leaps off the page, or his sentences and phrases, which are woven together to create a stellar example of fluency. No matter what trait you focus on, you and your students will love this book.

Focus Lessons for Developing Sentence Fluency

Focus Lesson Based On . . .

The Web Files
Margie Palatini, Author
Richard Egielski, Illustrator
Hyperion Press, 2001
(See description on page 115.)

Target Trait: Sentence Fluency
Secondary Traits: Word Choice, Voice

This laugh-out-loud book, written in the clipped, staccato style associated with detective writing, is perfect for Readers Theater. You can create scripts based on each of the story's characters, from "Ducktective Web" to "That Dirty Rat," and prepare students to perform for the class. Students hear the style as they perform and focus on the flow of the sentences, the influence of the words on fluency, and, of course, the marvelous voice.

Materials:

- A copy of *The Web Files*
- Scripts for each character from the book
- Signs for each of character made of $8^{1/2}$-by-11-inch paper with string for students to wear around their necks

What to Do:

1. Create scripts for each part by extracting lines of dialogue from the book and assigning roles to them—the sheep, the horse, Web, Bill, the narrator, and so on. Make signs for each character that students will wear, using 8 1/2-x-11-inch paper and pieces of string approximately 20 inches long.

2. Assign parts to students and give them a copy of the script and the appropriate sign. Some of the parts will contain tricky, tongue-twister passages, so assign those parts to readers who have lots of confidence. Let students read their parts silently before asking them to read them aloud.

3. Line performers up at the front of the room and have them read the script from beginning to end, with power and expression—stopping only for giggles.

4. When finished, pass out scripts to the students in the audience so everyone has a copy to read and discuss. Ask students if the performance was fluent. Make sure they give reasons to back up their answers.

Follow Up:

- Read other books written in detective style, such as *Tough Cookie* by David Wisniewski. Have students try out the style in their own writing.
- Videotape and show the opening credits of the TV show *Dragnet*. The old version runs in syndication. Discuss the script's style of writing and compare it to *The Web Files* or *Tough Cookie*. Make a list of other TV shows or movies written in this style.

Focus Lesson Based On . . .

Dream Weaver
Jonathan London, Author
Rocco Baviera, Illustrator
Harcourt, 1998
(See description on page 114.)

Target Trait: Sentence Fluency
Secondary Traits: Word Choice, Ideas

This text about spiders is so beautifully written that it begs to be read aloud. Filled with exquisite phrasing, students can read this book as a choral reading for the class to enjoy. A handy reference page at the end of the book contains information about spiders and how they live. In this lesson, students examine sentence fluency in the main text and compare it to the fluency of the reference page. They learn that sentence fluency varies according to the purpose of the writing.

Materials:

- A copy of *Dream Weaver* for each group of three students

What to Do:

1. Read *Dream Weaver* to students. Discuss the melody of the language.

2. Divide the class into groups of three and give each one a copy of *Dream Weaver*.

3. Assign each group a passage to read. Ask groups to read their passages aloud repeatedly until they are so familiar with them that they hardly need the book.

4. Ask groups to think about how they will read their passages aloud to the whole class. Tell them to think about where to raise and lower their voices, pause, and combine voices to create different moods. Let them practice for as long as necessary. Encourage students to add hand motions, dance, or music to enhance their reading.

5. Arrange the groups in a big circle so that that their parts mirror the organization of the text.

6. Have students read through the whole piece and, when they're finished, celebrate. Ask students which techniques they thought worked best and why.

7. Allow time for groups to revise their reading and present it to the class again. You will be amazed at the improvement! Discuss how this activity relates to sentence fluency in writing.

Follow Up:

- Use *Joyful Noise* by Paul Fleischman as another resource for reading aloud. It is already written out for two voices in parts and is popular with students as a paired reading.
- Use Gary Paulsen's *Dogteam* as a choral reading if you wish to use another text with marvelous sentence fluency for additional practice.

Focus Lesson Based On . . .

The Important Book
Margaret Wise Brown, Author
Leonard Weisgard, Illustrator
HarperCollins, 1999
(See description on page 109.)

Target Trait: Sentence Fluency
Secondary Traits: Organization, Ideas

The poems in this book use a pattern—a repeating first and last line. Each poem is slightly different in length, but follows the same bookend-type organization. For this lesson, students identify patterns in poems from *The Important Book*, create their own poems, and read them aloud.

MATERIALS:

- A copy of *The Important Book*
- Writing paper and pens or pencils

WHAT TO DO:

1. Read three poems from *The Important Book* aloud and ask students if they hear a pattern in each one that helps to make it flow smoothly. Students should easily note that the first and last line of every poem are the same.

2. Read another poem from the book, but this time, when you reach the last line, stop and ask students to call it out. They should know it because it will be the same as the first line. Repeat the process with different poems from the book until you feel students have grasped the pattern.

3. Discuss how a poem with a pattern like these from *The Important Book* can create fluency. Review the key elements of fluency—rhythm, cadence, and flow, and see if students can identify how Brown's poems achieve these elements.

4. Brainstorm a list of ideas for students to use to write their own poems: important people in their lives, important things learned in class that week, important things for students in their grade to know, and so on.

5. Ask students to write their own *Important Book* poems on topics of their choice. Invite students to read their poems aloud to the class.

FOLLOW UP:

- Create a class book and display in the library alongside a copy of Margaret Wise Brown's *The Important Book*.
- Compare *The Important Book* to Margaret Wise Brown's *Another Important Book* for sentence fluency. Are the poems constructed the same way or are they different?

Focus Lesson Based On . . .

John Henry

Julius Lester, Author

Jerry Pinkney, Illustrator

Puffin Books, 1994

(See description on page 114.)

Target Trait: Sentence Fluency

Secondary Traits: Word Choice, Voice

John Henry is an excellent book to study for fluency because of its sheer variety of well-written sentences. In this lesson, students read and analyze these sentences. They categorize them into simple, compound, complex, compound/complex, and fragment and look at how well the sentence variety works to create a story with energy and power.

Materials:

- Multiple copies of *John Henry*
- Overhead transparencies and markers
- Writing paper and pens or pencils

What to Do:

1. Read *John Henry* to students and discuss it. Tell students you are going to examine the book closely for the variety of sentences.

2. Organize the students into pairs. Give each pair a copy of *John Henry* and assign them a page from the book. Because there are 17 pages of text, you may need to assign two pages to some pairs to cover them all.

3. Ask the students to read the text on their page(s), examine each sentence, and categorize each one into one of these groups: (1) simple sentences, (2) compound sentences, (3) complex sentences, (4) compound/complex sentences, and (5) sentence fragments. Record how many types of each sentence are found. If necessary, review the basics of what each of these sentence types is, such as:

    - Simple: The sentence has only one independent clause. "The house is red."

- Compound: The sentence is composed of two independent clauses that are joined by a coordinating conjunction or a semicolon. "The house is red, but it is not the only red house on the block."
- Complex: The sentence is composed of one independent clause and one or more dependent clauses. "When I was leaving my red house, I realized I had forgotten to lock the door."
- Compound/Complex: The sentence is composed of a compound and a complex sentence. "The house is red, but it is not the only red house on the block, which is very confusing to people trying to find it for the first time."
- Fragment: An incomplete sentence used for stylistic effect. "A beautiful shade of red, like an overly ripe tomato."

4. As a class, ask the students to reveal how many sentences in each category they found and give examples. Tally the totals on the overhead for all students to see.

5. Discuss the impact of sentence variety on the overall fluency of a text, giving special emphasis to fragments and how to use them effectively.

Follow Up:

- Ask pairs of students to make a list of the different ways Lester starts sentences in *John Henry*.
- Encourage students to look at a piece of their own writing and revise it for sentence variety, using the different categories of sentences.

Focus Lesson Based On . . .

Hey You! C'mere: A Poetry Slam

Elizabeth Swados, Author

Joe Cepeda, Illustrator

Scholastic, 2002

(See description on page 117.)

Target Trait: Sentence Fluency

Secondary Traits: Word Choice, Voice, Ideas

Using poetry to help students bring sentence fluency to their own writing is a great idea. In this collection, you'll find poems that are tasty to read and interesting to hear. By carrying out the lesson, you'll show students how Swados uses "sound words" to add expression, rhythm, and cadence to her work and, in the process, show them how they might add it to their own work.

MATERIALS:

- A copy of *Hey You! C'mere*
- Overhead transparencies and markers
- Chart paper and pens
- Writing paper and pens or pencils
- Preprinted criteria forms for judging the poetry slam
- Bookbinding supplies: large white paper, magazines to be cut up, markers, pens, pencils, glue, tape, and scissors

WHAT TO DO:

1. Read *Hey You! C'mere* to students. Discuss the definition of a poetry slam with students: A poetry slam is the competitive form of poetry performance. Poets read poems aloud to an audience, focusing not only on what they're saying, but also on how they're saying it, and are rated by a panel of judges.

2. Ask students to name their favorite poems from *Hey You! C'mere*. Read these again, only this time ask students to listen for the fluency of the poems. Note how each poem contains descriptive words that incorporate sounds that invite expressive oral reading, such as "a slurp of spaghetti," ". . . kiss you, smooch you, koo-kootchie koo you," and "I hear his big, mean feet."

3. Have students identify food-related words in the poems, such as *spaghetti*, and list them on the overhead. Brainstorm sounds that go with each of these words. How does it sound when you eat this food? How does it sound when you cook, peel, or pick it? For *spaghetti*, you might say *slurp*, *smack*, *swish*, *snap*, and *crunch*.

4. Have students work in groups of three to select a food and write a poem about it. Let them brainstorm descriptive words and phrases to include in their poems. After they have at least ten words and phrases, ask the groups to write their poem.

5. Encourage students to read their drafts aloud as they write. When all groups have finished writing, tell them they are going to have a poetry slam. They may wish to continue writing and revising, knowing they will be competing with one another. If so, allow the time.

6. Arrange for older students, teachers, administrators, or parents to serve as judges for the poetry slam. Three is just the right number. Set the time and date for the slam, and tell students to have a final copy of their poems ready.

7. Ask students what criteria should be used for judging the poems. Write the criteria on chart paper and post the list in the front of the room so it is visible to students and judges. Assign points to each criterion so judges can differentiate the quality of the performances. Here is an example.

Criteria Scoring Sheet

Creativity: The poem revealed things about the topic that were out of the ordinary, interesting, and imaginative. (Ten points possible)

Fluency: The reading was smooth, rhythmic, and pleasing to the ear. (Ten points possible)

Word Choice and Voice: The poem had many interesting words that evoked strong feelings. (Ten points possible)

8. Allow students ample time to rehearse before the poetry slam.

9. Share the criteria with the judges ahead of time. Give them preprinted forms containing the criteria for scoring each group.

10. Let groups perform their poems. Give each group its scores at the end of the performance. Be sure to focus on what they did well along with areas for improvement. Declare the group with the highest score the winner of the poetry slam.

11. Celebrate all the poems by creating a collection, binding it, and leaving it out for all to read and enjoy.

Follow Up:

- Plan poetry slams on a regular basis. Choose different themes and have students either write their own poems or research existing poems on that theme.
- Challenge other classes to compete in future poetry slams with your students. Let your students teach other students how to write the poems and prepare for the slam.

Chapter Six

Strengthening Conventions

"The educational values of picture books go beyond content. Hearing and reading picture books, thinking about and working with them, can help children become better readers and writers."

—Susan Benedict and Lenore Carlisle
Beyond Words: Picture Books for Older Readers and Writers

Picture books are excellent for teaching students about conventions. Because, presumably, they've been through many rounds of editing before publication, the punctuation, grammar, and mechanics they contain should be accurate—and we can therefore use them as models of accuracy. But we should also use them to expose students to how authors use conventions in interesting and, occasionally, risky ways for stylistic reasons. For example, in *Hey You! C'mere: A Poetry Slam* by Elizabeth Swados, which we examined in Chapter 5, readers are treated to a book that uses conventions with panache.

"Chomp chomp, I'm naht suwposed to tawlk wid moy mudth fulled. Chomp chomp, itds bayad mahnners. Chomp chomp." Sophistication with conventions—that's the goal. We can use picture books to expose students to accurate and innovative uses of conventions and give them reasonable goals to reach for themselves.

All picture books, to some degree, can be used to teach about conventions. Students can look to picture books as mentor texts to model correctness in the five main areas of conventions: capitalization, punctuation, spelling, grammar and usage, and paragraphing. Certainly all of those mentioned in preceding chapters can be. They are prime examples of how authors flex their editing muscles, using conventions with style and accuracy. In this chapter, you will find more examples of books that will serve you and your students well as you study conventions.

Conventions: A Definition

Conventions allow us to edit the text and prepare it for the reader. The editing process makes the text understandable in a uniform way. If we believe that most writing is meant to be read by someone else, then we must use conventional standards to make the pieces as clear as possible. Almost anything a copyeditor deals with comes under the heading of conventions: spelling, punctuation, grammar and usage, capitalization, and paragraphing.

Here is a lesson based on a book that is written to celebrate punctuation, one of the five key areas that define the conventions trait.

FEATURE FOCUS LESSON BASED ON . . .

Punctuation Takes a Vacation
Robin Pulver, Author
Lynn Rowe Reed, Illustrator
Holiday House, 2003
(See description on page 132.)

Target Trait: Conventions
Secondary Traits: Word Choice, Ideas, Voice

This charming book helps students realize the importance of using punctuation well in their writing. Students show their understanding of punctuation by writing their own stories and postcards modeled after *Punctuation Takes a Vacation*.

MATERIALS:

- A copy of *Punctuation Takes a Vacation*
- A chapter book or textbook for every student
- Style books and other resources that have tips on how to use conventions correctly, such as textbooks, charts, reference guides, and handbooks
- Blank postcards
- Pens and pencils

WHAT TO DO:

Day 1:

1. Talk with students about the importance of punctuation. Why do we need it? How does correct punctuation make a piece easier to read?

2. Show students the different style books and other resources to help them with punctuation and the other conventions such as spelling, capitalization, paragraphing, and grammar.

3. Ask students what they think would happen if punctuation marks disappeared and we didn't use them anymore. Show a textbook or chapter book passage, and ask students to imagine how they would read it without punctuation.

4. Read *Punctuation Takes a Vacation*.

5. Have students write and illustrate postcards to each punctuation mark asking it to come back and explaining why they miss it.

6. Hang the postcards around the room so students can refer to them when they need to remember how to use punctuation correctly.

> *Send to:*
> *The Question Mark*
> *At Wondering Why Way*
> *Punctuationville, Anystate USA*
>
> *Dear Question Mark,*
>
> *I have a question to ask you, but since you are not here to go at the end of my question, I can't. I have so many questions about things like, "What's for lunch today", or "Can I have more allowance," but now I can't ask them because you're gone. PLEASE! PLEASE! come back. I promise to use you every day.*
>
> *Your inquisitive friend,*
> *Joseph*

Day 2:

1. Have students write a story similar to *Punctuation Takes a Vacation*, but focusing on parts of speech. What if all the nouns, verbs, or prepositions went on vacation? What would our writing look like without them? What would we miss most? What would we offer to do to get them back? Display these stories around the room.

2. Repeat the activity for spelling, capitalization, and paragraphing. By the time you are finished, students will have written enough stories to fill the room!

FOLLOW UP:

- Have the class develop its own "creative conventions handbook" that include pictures and paragraphs about punctuation and grammar rules written in an interesting, fun way.
- Create . . . *Takes a Vacation* books for content areas such as math (*Subtraction Takes a Vacation*, *Multiplication Takes a Vacation*, and so forth).

Picture Books for Strengthening Conventions

Words Are Categorical **series** (includes titles listed below)
Brian P. Cleary, Author
Carolrhoda Books

Dearly, Nearly, Insincerely: What Is an Adverb?
Brian Gable, Illustrator, 2003

Hairy, Scary, Ordinary: What Is an Adjective?
Jenya Prosmitsky, Illustrator, 2000

I and You and Don't Forget Who: What Is a Pronoun?
Brian Gable, Illustrator, 2004

A Mink, a Fink, a Skating Rink: What Is a Noun?
Jenya Prosmitsky, Illustrator, 2001

To Root, to Toot, to Parachute: What Is a Verb?
Jenya Prosmitsky, Illustrator, 2001

Under, Over, By the Clover: What Is a Preposition?
Brian Gable, Illustrator, 2003

These picture books are just what you need to help students understand parts of speech. Each one is short, clever, and very colorful, and contains catch phrases that students can memorize and use as triggers when they write. You can use them, too, as you talk with students to help them revise and edit their work. You might say, "Remember *A Mink, a Fink, a Skating Rink*, Franco. Read the paragraph you just wrote and see if it has enough specific and interesting nouns in it." Or, "Emily, *Under, Over, By the Clover!* You may have gone overboard with prepositions in your story about armadillos. Read it again and cut some prepositional phrases to make your writing more specific." Finding interesting and effective tools to teach conventions is a challenge. But the job will be easier if you add these books to your classroom library.

***World of Language* series** (includes titles listed below)

Ruth Heller, Author and Illustrator

Putnam & Grosset Group

***Behind the Mask: A Book About Prepositions,* 1998**

***A Cache of Jewels and Other Collective Nouns,* 1998**

***Fantastic! Wow! and Unreal! A Book About Interjections and Conjunctions,* 2000**

***Kites Sail High: A Book About Verbs,* 1998**

***Many Luscious Lollipops: A Book About Adjectives,* 1998**

***Merry-Go-Round: A Book About Nouns,* 1998**

***Mine, All Mine: A Book About Pronouns,* 1999**

***Up, Up, and Away: A Book About Adverbs,* 1998**

These books are a gold mine for teachers who want to teach language in a colorful, engaging, and unique way. Each book focuses on a different part of speech or element of grammar, providing rules and examples that students can easily understand and apply to their own writing.

The series works well as a bridge between the word choice trait and the conventions trait. Every time we show connections from one trait to another, we help students see the big picture of what they should be trying to achieve in their writing and the skills needed to accomplish their goals.

Grammar Tales

Scholastic, 2004

Chicken in the City (Nouns)
Maria Fleming, Author; Kelly Kennedy, Illustrator

A Verb for Herb (Verbs)
Maria Fleming, Author; Doug Jones, Illustrator

The Bug Book (Adjectives)
Maria Fleming, Author; Gary Swift, Illustrator

Tillie's Tuba (Adverbs)
Maria Fleming, Author; Doug Jones, Illustrator

The Planet Without Pronouns (Pronouns)
Justin McCory Martin, Author; Jared Lee, Illustrator

The Mega-Deluxe Capitalization Machine (Capitalization)
Justin McCory Martin, Author;
Matt Phillips, Illustrator

When Comma Came to Town (Commas)
Liza Charlesworth, Author; Doug Jones, Illustrator

The Mystery of the Missing Socks (Quotation Marks)
Justin McCory Martin, Author;
Kelly Kennedy, Illustrator

The No-Good, Rotten, Run-On Sentence (Sentence Structure)
Liza Charlesworth, Author; Doug Jones, Illustrator

Francine Fribble, Proofreading Policewoman (Proofreading)
Justin McCory Martin, Author; Jared Lee, Illustrator

Each title in Scholastic's Grammar Tales series is written with a clever spin on a conventions skill that is bound to make kids smile. From Francine Fribble, Proofreading Policewoman to Steve Scoop the reporter for the Hoopletown Evening Herald, every character is on the case to make editing a lively and exacting adventure. Every book can stand alone, but you'd be missing a wonderful teaching and learning tool not to have the whole series available for students of all ages.

Letter Writer Starter Set

Nancy Cobb, Author

Laura Cornell, Illustrator

The Reader's Digest Children's Books, 1999

Here is the perfect book to use when teaching conventions, particularly conventions associated with letter writing. It includes tips, hints, and detailed directions of what to capitalize, how to punctuate, and other issues that arise when writing letters. It is lively, informative, and very practical. The nuts and bolts of letter writing are fully explored here. You will love this book and all the goodies it contains—stickers, envelopes, writing paper, and lists of ideas to make letters better.

If You Were a Writer

Joan Lowery Nixon, Author

Bruce Degen, Illustrator

Four Winds Press, 1988

Here is another book that is worthy of your collection. It teaches students about the writing process in a highly engaging way. Nixon uses a dialogue between a mother and her daughter to show how writers puzzle through many of the difficult parts of the writing process to come up with good stories. Students can study it to learn how to use dialogue to inform and explain.

Punctuation Takes a Vacation

Robin Pulver, Author

Lynn Rowe Reed, Illustrator

Holiday House, 2003

What if one day punctuation marks became fed up with being misused and abused and decided to take a vacation? Once they are gone, students in the story realize how hard it is to communicate clearly without them. The punctuation marks write witty postcards to the students, reminding them of how important they are. Of course, in the end, the students and punctuation marks happily reunite. See focus lesson on page 127.

Yo! Yes?

Chris Raschka, Author and Illustrator

Scholastic, 1993

Two boys meet and explore the possibilities for a friendship by asking and answering simple questions: "Yo!" "Yes?" Communicating with few words, the story unfolds with clever use of punctuation marks to show how the characters interact using inflection, questions, and emphatic statements. Without the clever use of conventions throughout, the central idea would be lost on the reader. Students can borrow the idea from this book and make their own expressive stories that center on the creative use of conventions to create meaningful text.

Down the Road

Alice Schertle, Author

E.B. Lewis, Illustrator

Harcourt, 1995

Aside from the fact that this is a "fine book that speaks straight to the heart," according to *Booklist*, it is a prime example of dialogue used well. Schertle relies heavily on conversation. She demonstrates excellent paragraphing and applies sophisticated punctuation. A student learning how to write dialogue would greatly benefit from studying the use of quotation marks in this book. Put this book in students' hands and see if it doesn't help them work out some of the trickier issues of punctuation, capitalization, and paragraphing in dialogue.

Children of the Earth . . . Remember

Schim Schimmel, Author and Illustrator

NorthWord, 1997

Simple, elegant prose lights up this book. Conventions are not the first thing that come to mind, and that's good. You hear the message of this piece through the author's powerful use of language, the voice that rings true on every page, and the poignant environmental theme to save the earth for future generations. None of these things would shine as brightly, however, without Schimmel's quiet use of correct conventions on every page. It's a good lesson for students—that conventions support the text and shouldn't be the first thing that readers notice. This lovely story of Mother Earth is an excellent example of conventions used well.

Beverly Billingsly Borrows a Book

Alexander Stadler, Author and Illustrator

Harcourt, 2002

Every person who worries about a library fine, an overdue book, or just worries in general loves this book. As Stadler tells Beverly's story, notice his fine use of conventions to enhance the dialogue. Other conventions are highlighted here, too, such as capitalization of dialogue and proper nouns, including some long and complex dinosaur names. This book is delightful to read both for content and mechanics.

Looking at text as an editor does is a process worth teaching. Each time students recognize a skill that someone else has handled well, they take a step closer to applying that skill in their own work. That's our goal for teaching conventions—getting students to edit their own work like pros.

CHAPTER SEVEN

Spotlighting Presentation

"In looking at picture books, adults see first the actions which advance the story. Children tend to see the odd things—the frog sitting in the shadow of the wall, the picture of two cows, the horse running outside of the open window, the torn pocket, the cracked window."

—Welleran Poltarnes
Sharing the Pleasures of Reading

Can you use picture books to teach presentation? Sure! Why not? You will find every possible visual element in the world in picture books. And because presentation is all about appearance, picture books are a suitable way to help students learn how to make their text appealing to the reader's eye.

We can help students read the pictures right along with the text. The presentation of the text is designed to convey meaning. The use of contrasting color and repeating images bring forth the important ideas in Ed Young's *Three Blind Mice*. Wordless picture book stories such as *Sector 7* by David Wiesner are organized naturally with no written text to support them—all through pictures. The voice of *Fox* by Margaret Wild is clear from the design of the first page; it's sharp and jarring. The whimsical drawings in *Wolf!* by Becky Bloom support our interpretation of funny words and catchy phrases in the text. In *Behold the Trees* by Sue

Alexander, the beauty of the phrasing is mirrored in the magnificence of the illustrations. We learn important lessons about the value of conventions in *Punctuation Takes a Vacation*. Presentation is the trait where the pictures and the words intersect. When done well, they work together seamlessly to create meaning for the reader.

Presentation: A Definition

Presentation is the final piece of the writing trait puzzle. How the writing looks to the reader is at its heart. Good writers are aware of the importance of presentation. Final copy can serve as a welcome mat or as a barricade to the reader, depending on the level of care the writer has taken. In picture books, the presentation is, in great measure, a product of a gifted illustrator working in harmony with the ideas of the author. How well the text and illustrations support each other is one of the keys to a successful picture book.

What follows are some picture books that caught my eye for presentation from the lists of books in earlier sections. They are a visual smorgasbord. As you review these books and others, remember that when a book is presented well it:

- Is pleasing to the eye
- Is appealing and inviting
- Is formatted for readability
- Is interesting and worthy of note
- Works in harmony with the text to create meaning

FEATURE FOCUS LESSON BASED ON . . .

Over the Moon
Rachel Vail, Author
Scott Nash, Illustrator
Scholastic, 1998
(See description on page 140.)

Focus Trait: Presentation
Secondary Traits: Ideas, Voice, Word Choice

Quiet on the set! We're filming a classic nursery rhyme here, but that darn cow just doesn't understand that she's supposed to jump over the moon, not through it, under it, or next to it. Hi Diddle Diddle, the director of this classic rhyme, has his work cut out for him if he's ever going to get this right. Resembling a comic book in its presentation, dialogue boxes are used to showcase the lively spoken text throughout the piece. In this lesson, students will create their own stories based on nursery rhymes and use dialogue boxes when characters speak.

MATERIALS:

- A copy of *Over the Moon* for each small group of three to four students
- Copies of Mother Goose nursery rhymes such as "Humpty Dumpty," "Jack and Jill," "Little Miss Muffet," "The Little Old Lady Who Lived in a Shoe," and so on
- Drawing paper, pens, pencils, and markers

WHAT TO DO:

1. Read *Over the Moon* and show the illustrations as you go.
2. Discuss how the main character in the piece—the cow—causes problems for the director by not following the standard nursery rhyme. The cow won't go over the moon; she'll go under it, through it, around it, but not over.
3. Pass out copies of *Over the Moon* to small groups and let them look closely at the illustrations. Point out that the dialogue is in text boxes in this book, a format that students may recognize if they read comic strips.
4. Assign each group a different Mother Goose nursery rhyme. Read each one aloud in small groups.
5. Ask each group to figure out a twist they can write into a new version of their nursery rhyme. For example: Humpty Dumpty may not be willing to fall off the wall. Little Miss Muffet may not want to sit on a tuffet (a small stool). Maybe the Little Old Lady who lives in the shoe gets evicted because she has so many children.
6. Allow time for students to write their new nursery rhymes. Make sure they include conversation between characters as part of their text. Share the new version aloud to the whole group. Revise as needed.
7. Write final copies of the new nursery rhymes on the drawing paper, using dialogue boxes to frame the spoken parts. Encourage students to use creativity to make the dialogue boxes as effective as possible. For example, if a character yells out, the box should be bigger. If several characters are talking at once, the boxes can intersect.

Display the finished new pieces on a bulletin board for all students to enjoy.

FOLLOW UP:

- Assign parts to students from their text, and have them act out the story. Everything written in a text box is a spoken part; the rest of the text would be read by a narrator.
- Put on a Nursery Rhyme Festival and share the stories in written form along with their performances.

Picture Books for Spotlighting Presentation

Behold the Trees

Sue Alexander, Author

Leonid Gore, Illustrator

Scholastic, 2001

Watercolor wonderful, this book is a treat to the eyes. It's rich and luxurious in color and texture.

The Magic Fan

Keith Baker, Author and Illustrator

Voyager Books, 1984

The blend of story, artistry, and format is spellbinding. The way the text works with the fold-out pictures is sheer genius.

Wolf!

Becky Bloom, Author

Pascal Biet, Illustrator

Orchard Books, 1999

The illustrations here are lots of fun, just like the book. This book makes you laugh. It's clever and the pictures contain many little details that add to the book's original idea.

The Important Book

Margaret Wise Brown, Author

Leonard Weisgard, Illustrator

HarperCollins, 1999

Here is an example of a traditional picture book, looking just as it did when it was first published in 1949.

Night of the Gargoyles

Eve Bunting, Author

David Wiesner, Illustrator

Dark and a touch on the creepy side, the illustrations and the text's layout are sure to intrigue the reader.

Home Run

Robert Burleigh, Author

Mike Wimmer, Illustrator

Harcourt, 1998

The illustrations are a perfect complement to this book's ideas. They work together to create a bigger understanding of the topic.

Beware of Storybook Wolves

Lauren Child, Author and Illustrator

Scholastic, 2000

Handwritten and typed text, large to small print, and accents enhance the whimsical voice of this story.

Blood & Gore

Vicki Cobb, Author and Illustrator

Scholastic, 1997

This book proves it: Nonfiction can be fascinating and accessible.

The Spider and the Fly

Tony DiTerlizzi, Author and Illustrator

Simon and Schuster, 2002

This updated version of the traditional tale is done in a black-and-white, take-your-breath-away style. Quite worthy of the 2002 Caldecott Medal.

How Are You Peeling?

Saxton Freymann and Joost Elffers, Authors

Scholastic, 1999

Brightly colored photographs of humanized fruits and vegetables make this an eye-catching book.

Don't Take Your Snake for a Stroll

Karin Ireland, Author

David Catrow, Illustrator

Harcourt, 2003

This book, a wild kaleidoscope of color and craziness, will be a favorite with students.

Cloud Dance

Thomas Locker, Author and Illustrator

Voyager Books, 2000

Exquisite paintings and a beautifully descriptive text are hallmarks of this book and others by Locker.

Who's Got Game? The Ant or the Grasshopper?

Toni Morrison and Slade Morrison, Authors

Pascal Lemaitre, Illustrator

Scribner, 2003

Cartoonlike drawings, speech bubbles, and lots of color draw the reader into this great new version of the familiar Aesop tale.

Rose's Journal: The Story of a Girl in the Great Depression

Marissa Moss, Author

Harcourt, 2001

Students will enjoy this book because it looks like a young writer really wrote and illustrated it.

Charlie Parker Played Be Bop

Chris Raschka, Author and Illustrator

Scholastic, 1992

Using the shape of the letters and their sizes, the author replicates the sound of jazz in the simple, musical text.

A Bad Case of Stripes

David Shannon, Author and Illustrator

Scholastic, 1998

Bold and bodacious, this text takes some big risks with its use of color and dramatic illustrations.

Rimshots

Charles R. Smith Jr., Author and Illustrator

Penguin Putnam Books, 1999

Each page is a visual delight in this book of poems, stories, and interesting bits about basketball.

Over the Moon

Rachel Vail, Author

Scott Nash, Illustrator

Scholastic, 1998

Resembling a comic book, this book features dialogue boxes to highlight spoken text, an easily replicable technique for students.

The Z Was Zapped

Chris Van Allsburg, Author and Illustrator

Walter Lorraine Books, 1987

Van Allsburg's black-and-white illustrations go far beyond the text to communicate this piece's intriguing idea.

Fox

Margaret Wild, Author

Ron Brooks, Illustrator

Kane/Miller Publishers, 2001

I found this book to be haunting and even a bit scary. It's not for young children. The stylized print and illustrations along with the story leave you with an unsettled feeling long after the last page is turned.

The Secret Knowledge of Grown-Ups

David Wisniewski, Author and Illustrator

Lothrop, Lee & Shepard, 1998

The combination of paper collage and use of color, along with wildly imaginative ideas, make this a stand-out book.

The Other Side

Jacqueline Woodson, Author

Earl B. Lewis, Illustrator

G.P. Putnam's Sons, 2001

There is a graceful elegance to this book that is enhanced by its realistic illustrations of people in a place we all recognize: our own backyard.

Seven Blind Mice

Ed Young, Author and Illustrator

Philomel Books, 1992

The use of black as a background in this book makes each page a standout. Each page is a collage of color, shape, and design that is masterfully presented.

From fiction to nonfiction, picture books are outstanding resources for your students to learn about presentation. Read these books with an eye toward helping students understand how the art and illustration enhance the author's ideas. Help them notice how sometimes the text melts into the pictures. Explain that, in good picture books, the illustrations and the text work together hand in hand, drawing the reader in.

Author Index

Title Index